MY PIMP WIFE

How My Loving Japanese Wife Evolved Into A Cold, Heartless Pimp

ERIC CULPEPPER

CONTAINS ADULT LANGUAGE

In The Wind Productions

Publisher: In The Wind Productions

ISBN: 978-1-5331274-0-2
ISBN: 1-5331274-0-9

CONTENTS

ABOUT THE COVER

THE IMAGE ON the cover of this book is a multitasking Asian woman, which very poignantly represents the various dimensions of greed, hatred, hyper-industrialization, ultra-feminism and, subsequently, my wife's mental disposition.

MY PIMP WIFE

How My Loving Japanese Wife Evolved Into A Cold, Heartless Pimp

ERIC CULPEPPER

CONTAINS ADULT LANGUAGE

INTRO

MY PIMP WIFE is the raw, lasciviously juicy international tale of how my loving wife evolved into a cold, heartless pimp and the core primary reason that I chose to write this book is that, as a Grand Inquisitor Level Pimpnological Decryptologist, in the public interest, I wanted to write about one of the more common, yet rarely recognized, ominous aspects of earnestly aspiring to be a true master pimp.

MEETING MOMMY

THE BEGINNING OF this lurid inter-continental adventure finds me as a 19 year old kid obliviously ice skating at The Mall Of Memphis in the Summer of 1988. At this point in my life, I had just been ripped off by a trucking school and I was experiencing the unspeakably unpleasant experience of attempting to date in North America.

During this time, I spent every spare moment ice skating at the mall and I happened to meet a Japanese university post-graduate ESL student named Masa and a small group of his fellow ESL students.

I was also beginning to, once again, experience some of the more rarely acknowledged and discussed aspects of the phenomena of pussy power.

For example, there was a girl named Jody that I went to junior high school with, as students, Jody was just another face in the crowd that I absolutely did not get along with. As a matter of fact, given that Black women are so obsessed with the idea of being totally hideous so-called strong, totally independent, Black women there were a lot of young women that I didn't get along with in junior high school, which I often refer to as, the age of cruelty because children at that age take such immense pleasure in bullying and degrading as many other students as they can . . .

However, that was never, ever a problem for me, because I was very good at thinking that low-lives were totally irrelevant and their completely worthless opinions meant absolutely and completely nothing to me, not to mention the fact that I was soberly aware of the fact that I was completely surrounded by a group of people that, upon graduation, I would very likely never ever see again in life . . . Which suited me just fine in several cases.

However, all of this is not to say that I did not enjoy attending junior high school, I in fact did enjoy junior high school to the point that, given that I completely hated attending school in general, enjoying junior high school became suspicious to me to the point that it required some in-depth analysis in which I concluded that, we were quite literally being tricked into running to school everyday because the vast majority of our instructors were forty plus year veteran educators who had educated us, and most of our parents, as children instead of trying to force us to be the highly focused adults that we were not . . . Which became quite helpful when I quite unexpectedly became an ESL educator of kindergarten, elementary and junior high school students myself in a foreign country.

Some of the things that I immensely enjoyed about being a student at an all Black junior high school, aside from rarely succeeding at trying to talk my way out of my daily ass-whipping by my civics teacher for being a highly accomplished class clown and grinding on some of my more voluptuous classmates, was racing the entire school of young negro boys to lunch, which was a highly intense daily race in which I only just barely managed to make it first once in three years because I had to run from the completely opposite end of the building. However, being first in line to lunch, just that once, was so exhilarating that I still feel an extremely great sense of accomplishment, even at the age of forty.

Jody and I didn't go to the same high school, however, somehow I encountered her several times and we wound up exchanging phone numbers, visiting each other, meeting each-other's parents, going to the movies together and I even somehow managed to wind up with Jody's picture in my wallet . . . Which guys at work said was extremely nice, which kind of made me take a second and even third look at her photo.

An interesting episode of my various experiences with Jody is that, one day, when I was about 19, I was at home and I had a migraine headache and Jody called me and told me that she wanted me to come over to her place and I told her that I really didn't feel well.

I guess that she told me that she would make me feel better because I wound up driving over to her house and when I got there I discovered that the real reason that she had called me was because she was extremely horny and she wanted to have sex with me . . . But she didn't tell me this when I walked in the door.

When I walked in, she gave me something to drink and a kiss on the cheek and she invited me up to her room where she undressed me and attempted to quite literally molest me. It had in fact been quite a long time since I had had a teenaged girl undress me and completely have her way with me . . . I hadn't experienced such ecstasy since I lost my virginity to my teenaged babysitters when I was in kindergarten.

However, the problem was that, since I was an extremely healthy and well-endowed teenager and neither of us had any real experience sexually, I was so big that I could not get into her vagina and she eventually got mad and gave up . . .

After I eventually left, as I drove home my head started hurting again and I realized that the moment that I got out of the car and walked in her front door my migraine headache completely disappeared and it didn't come back until I had made it back home again . . . What had that pussy done to me?

Like any total dumbass young woman, Jody started dating thugs, whom she found far more exciting and attractive than people who stayed out of shit and worked for a living.

During our long hiatus from seeing each other I was introduced to a Japanese lady named Takako.

Though I initially thought that she was 17, Takako was in fact a 25 year old Japanese economics graduate from Minamata, Japan, a place that I had never heard of before and therefore never even remotely imagined was a fact that would one day completely destroy everything that I had ever loved and worked for in my entire adult life.

My days with Takako and her fellow ESL students were by far some of the happiest days of my life. It seemed as though there wasn't a single day that passed that we didn't all put in $10.00 each, buy tons of food and drinks and bar-b-que together. Since she didn't have a car, I became Takako's chauffeur and we went absolutely everywhere and spent every sleeping and waking moment together and I was naturally starting to like her and develop feelings for her . . .

What I wasn't sure about, however, was the fact that she wasn't very voluptuous like Black men generally like women, but, she also wasn't a total wacko like Black men generally experienced women, so given the choice between a total nut job with a big ole butt and a bad attitude and a super nice Asian lady with an average figure, I took the smaller ride, rather than one of the big crazy ones.

When I eventually asked Takako to be my girlfriend, the very disappointing answer was a firm, " No, I can't be your girlfriend, because you're too young!" As a matter of fact, I was younger than her youngest sister . . . However, she was willing to be friends, which kept us literally glued together every day . . .

Though I was quite disappointed, as her chauffeur, we were still cruising around daily and soon it was her who was developing feelings for me . . . Especially, after she started curiously probing me and rubbing my hair and studying me more closely and I eventually kissed her . . . It was one of the most wonderful experiences of both of our lives, as it continued to be for the full length of what would eventually be our more than two decade long relationship.

We eventually spent so much time together that without knowing it we just literally melded into a couple. Just before we met, I had lost my dad to a freak car accident and I used the small portion of what my grandmother had determined was my share of the insurance settlement that I eventually got to buy Takako some clothes and a small television for her dorm. Takako appreciated those clothes so much that she literally wore them for years, even after we no longer lived in America, and when she eventually had to move out of her dorm for a couple of months, I told her that I was sure that it would be perfectly ok with my grandfather if she stayed at our house and by the time that we moved out of that house we had been there for eight years and had had three children together.

I can recall that when she first moved in and started washing my clothes and cooking for me, completely without me asking or even thinking of her washing my clothes and cooking for me, she asked me if I liked rice . . .

I can remember telling her that I absolutely hated rice because it was nasty . . . Then she went into this huge lecture about the innumerable breeds of rice and how it was just American rice that tasted horrible and once we were able to get our hands on some good rice I would totally love it and we eventually got our hands on what I didn't know was some of the best rice in the World and I totally loved it.

Takako managed to get along extremely well with my grandfather and sister, who absolutely loved her, and she even got along with my grandfather's hideous sister, who unfortunately lived right next door.

Though our lives were dreamy, there was one scare from her family.

The phone rang one day and it was a very anxious sounding international operator, "Does Takako live here," she asked anxiously?

"Yes, she does," I answered.

"Could you put her on the phone?"

"Sure," I said.

"Takako," I called out . . . While listening to someone chatter on the phone in an incomprehensible language.

"I think that it's from Japan," I told her . . . As I gave her the receiver.

"Oka san," she exclaimed loudly!

"It's my mother," she told me.

They had a seemingly intense conversation for about 15 minutes and then she hung up the phone and told me, "That was my mother, she thought that I had been kidnapped and when I told her that I was living with my boyfriend she told me to pack all of my things and come home immediately."

"Oh dear," I told her. "I never thought about anyone thinking that you had been kidnapped."

"It's ok," she told me . . . "My parents are very prejudice and they always worry . . . Before I came to America, they told me not to get involved with a Black man and now that I have, my father is angry, but my sister Yuko, who told me to find a husband in America, is very, very happy for me."

I was very, very happy too to finally have a super-awesome woman who wasn't an absolute and complete psycho . . . In fact, Takako was so even tempered that I literally couldn't wait to get into her pants, just to see if she was really a woman and when I found that she actually was a woman I absolutely couldn't believe it. I had literally never in my life met a woman under the age of sixty who wasn't absolutely and completely fucking insane, especially when they were menstruating.

After about six months, we started sleeping together and Takako eventually became pregnant with both our first child. About halfway into her pregnancy, Takako started insisting that we get married, I believed in marriage, but I had seen so much divorce and so many couples part that I felt that we would stay together far longer if we remained extremely good friends who lived together . . .

"No," Takako said . . . "If we're having a baby together, we must get married," so seeing as how she was extremely determined to get married and actually stay married and how much I really and truly loved her combined with the slim chance of me ever meeting a woman that possessed even an iota of sanity, on the advice of my grandfather, instead of having a huge ceremony, we went down to the courthouse and got married . . . We could always have a large traditional wedding ceremony later if we liked.

When the judge saw us walking toward him with her stomach sticking out, he already knew what we wanted and we were able to get a broom from a janitor, jump over it in the old slave tradition and we were officially married.

However, being a nineteen year old kid, I was $20.00 short of the fee to get married and I had to go back home and get $20.00 from my grandfather and bring it back to the courthouse to get our official marriage license.

For the most part, Takako thoroughly enjoyed her first pregnancy, I would occasionally see her smiling and hugging her stomach when she felt the baby kicking . . . Being impregnated was a deeply satisfying experience for her, especially given that she had never had a boyfriend before.

One day I came home from being out taking care of business of some sort and when I entered the door, Takako told me that Jody had called and said that she was coming over, even though Takako had told her that I was not at home.

I was quite surprised, I hadn't talked to Jody in months and she almost never called me, it was always me who had called her . . . I had absolutely no idea of what was going on, I thought that her mother had died or something.

Within a few moments, sure enough, the doorbell rang, I looked out of the door and it was Jody . . .

I was like, "Jody, what are you doing here, I haven't seen or heard from you in months . . . Has something happened?"

"I just wanted to see your new wife," she retorted!

"How did you know that I had a wife?"

"I called you to see how you were doing and a foreign woman answered the phone and I knew that she was your wife . . ."

"And I see that she's pregnant . . . Congratulations," she said sarcastically as she abruptly left!

When we eventually made it to the delivery room I was a nervous wreck to the point that Takako grabbed me by the arm and said, "Why are you so scared, I'm the one who is having the baby?!"

I told her that a childhood friend of mine had lost his mother in childbirth, she had actually died having him and it had always haunted me . . .

If my wife had died delivering our child I would have dropped dead on the spot . . .

Mommy lived, however, we did not manage to escape tragedy . . . Though we took the absolute best of care of our new baby, we unfortunately lost her to SIDS, commonly known as Crib Death and when we did, both our mothers did not take the news of the loss of their first grandchild very well. As a matter of fact, they both told us in two different languages from two different corners of the world that we didn't know what we were doing and that is why we had lost our first daughter . . .

We were inconsolably depressed . . . However, we eventually had two other daughters who brought us a tremendous amount of joy in both their youth and infancy and when our third daughter turned about two years old, Takako's mother and sister came over to visit their first niece and granddaughter.

When Takako's mother arrived in America, we rented a large sedan to take them places, because both my grandfather and I had pickup trucks . . .

My grandfather absolutely would not buy me a Cadillac or any other Pimp-mobile type of vehicle because he had in fact adopted us from the state when my mother lost us because of her totally relentless strong, totally independent, Black female hideousness that nearly landed her in federal prison for every kind of senselessness under the sun. And since grandfather knew that I had literally been raised by Pimps, which all started at his chain of restaurants when I was a toddler and our restaurant catered largely to night-lifers, he thought that I might get myself in trouble if he bought me too big of a car.

My grandfather's astoundingly hideous sister had a big coupe, but she acted such a huge idiot when anybody asked her to drive it that it in fact just sat there and rotted . . . Especially, after she created a huge scene years earlier when I had asked her to use it to take Jody out on a date and she came over and cursed me out in front of Jody which caused Jody to get totally pissed off at me because I didn't curse my grandfather's sister back out right in front of my grandfather.

Who does that?

Jody criticized me for months behind that, however, my grandfather was so proud of me having real sensibility that Black women have proven time and time again that they absolutely do not possess that he bought me a Chevy

Silverado pickup truck and firmly chastened me to never ever ask his sister for anything ever again . . . And I never did.

When Takako's mother made it to the house, she did a thorough inspection of the entire house, including the fact that we weren't living alone, we were living with my grandfather, which she highly approved of . . . We had two 50 pound bags of high grade rice, check. We had plenty of food in the deep freezer and refrigerator, check . . . And she also inspected her grandchildren, who spoke fluent Japanese as their first language, final check . . . We passed the inspection, with the exception of Takako tossing my keys down to me, at my request... Her mother did not approve of her throwing things at her husband.

After that, it was off to inspect a few restaurants, during which her mother made me laugh by screwing the caps off of several of the seasonings that she encountered and smelling them . . . I think that she was pretty pleased with what she saw, until someone served her some Miso Soup, she smelled it and took one sip, made a highly perturbed facial expression and absolutely refused to eat it . . . check. No pass for the sub-par Japanese-American Miso soup...

Her sister was pretty much enjoying the trip and the girls took to their aunt and grandmother like they had spent their entire lives together, which it had been planned that they eventually would, because I sure wasn't having them raised with the totally witless, strong, totally independent, Black women who had spent more than half of a Century claiming that they didn't need anybody which had quite literally turned Black America into a huge slum.

Takako told me that her sister was completely shocked at how loud people were at restaurants. Which caused me to be shocked, I told her that we hadn't even been to any loud restaurants, we went to an upscale Japanese restaurant in Memphis that we frequented and we went to a pretty quiet Pizza Hut in Hot Springs, Arkansas.

If they found these places shocking, what would they think of a really loud restaurant in a place like say, Baltimore or Boston, where, especially the Black kids are extremely high decibel.

Her family stayed for about a week and wrapped up their trip and went back to The Land Of The Rising Sun, which I think ultimately made our eventual move to Japan easier since her family at least had some familiarity with our children.

THE KOKO INCIDENT

ONE DAY, TAKAKO told me that she had a Japanese lady friend who needed to go to a small town down in Mississippi to get her things that she had left there when she moved to Memphis. Given that I absolutely loved taking road trips and Takako knew that I would do anything for her, we loaded this young lady named KoKo, who spoke very broken English and said that she had been a hostess, up in my pickup and we headed down to Itta Bena, Mississippi.

When we got down to this little town there were a lot of people walking around and she said that several of them were wearing her clothes. Takako and I were quite shocked . . .

She jumped out of the pickup, ran into a shotgun shack of a house and grabbed a small suitcase and a couple of boxes and then she ran back out and jumped in the truck and said, "Let's go!..." Like she was scared of something, so I put the Silverado in gear and we got the hell out of there and we've never been back.

On the way back to Memphis, she starts telling us all of these tales about how her boyfriend sometimes grabbed her by her beautiful waist length hair and slammed her head into the refrigerator and dresser when he was mad at her . . . But she kept saying that he was a really nice guy once you get to know him and we should meet him sometime . . . With both our eyes bulging in stunned disbelief at what we were hearing, we very kindly passed on the invitation the meet this psycho that she had come from Japan with.

I asked her if she ever thought about going back to Japan and she said that she couldn't return to Japan because her boyfriend wouldn't let her have her passport and she said that her relationship with her parents had been totally destroyed because her parents were totally against her going to America with a stranger in the first place and after he started abusing her, her parents had sent her the money to come home three times, but each time her boyfriend would make up with her and they would spend the money until her parents wouldn't send her any more money to come home.

When we got back to Memphis, we dropped KoKo off in front of an apartment building and we wished her well and went back home. After we had dinner, we discussed how unfortunate Koko's situation was and what we might be able to do to help her before we went off to bed.

At about 3 a.m. in the morning, I sprung to an upright position out of a literal death of sleep, my mind was racing as I had somehow figured out in my sleep that KoKo's boyfriend was in fact a Pimp who had lured her far away from home to America and was using some very common Pimp tactics to completely isolate KoKo and eventually break and Pimp her.

I was so shocked by what I had figured out that I was literally talking to myself to the point that Takako was awakened from a literal death of sleep . . . With groggy, cat like, sleepy Asian eyes, she was like, "What's wrong, why aren't you sleeping?"

I told Takako what I had figured out about KoKo's boyfriend being a Pimp, as far as I knew, she had never even heard the word Pimp before and she was completely stunned and not totally convinced that I knew what I was talking about, however, I assured her that I had been exposed to such things for many years and I absolutely did know precisely what I was talking about.

Later in the morning, when my grandfather awoke, I told him what I had figured out and concluded, my grandfather had run a chain of night restaurants that almost solely catered to Pimps for forty years, he believed me.

I told him that I thought that I should at least tell her what was going on so that she could somehow protect herself from this Gorilla Pimp . . . which is the lowest ranking and most irrational Pimp in the ancient hierarchy of Pimps.

At our first opportunity, Takako and I went back over to the apartment where we had dropped her off and no one there had ever seen or heard of her, she had quite literally disappeared into thin air and we have never again seen her.

THE DEATH OF GOD

FOR YEARS ON end, my relationship with Takako never hit a speed bump until I tried to teach her how to drive . . .

There is something very strange and telling about the flow of driving that brings out the hidden truth about people and just as you can tell what kind of mother a young girl will be by how she treats her dolls, you can likewise tell what kind of psycho someone is by how they drive their car.

Takako and I had never had a disagreement about anything, but telling her how to drive a car properly triggered something in her that completely pissed her off and made her act completely crazy . . . I had never seen that side of her before and after years together, I was dumb enough to think that it didn't exist . . . But I stopped teaching her how to drive and we got over it and I simply concluded that she didn't like anyone telling her how to do anything . . . However, just as comfort has the ability to destroy a relationship, I was slowly, but surely, beginning to see another side of her.

Even though we had managed to get along so well for so long and I am not a chauvinistic or controlling person on any level, Takako gradually reached the point that she wouldn't listen to anything that I told her, no matter how great the level of practicality of my instructions . . .

For example, being an extremely highly family oriented individual, I took my family on the road with me as often as I possibly could. On one of those innumerable road trips, I had a load into the Bronx with an astoundingly shitty trucking outfit that eventually went out of business for every violation under the sun and then a few violations beyond that.

When a business is exceptionally trashy, every aspect of its maintenance, operation and consumer base are invariably likewise trashy.

When the family and I pulled into the belly of hell to unload our shipment, there appeared to be a pretty big construction project going on in the area, because half of the cobblestones were missing in the cobblestone street that we were on and there were areas of the street that had been sealed off with cones and orange tape.

The building that we were backing into was located under a section of New York's elevated train line and we had to do quite a bit of maneuvering to get backed in to the door that I had been assigned to without damaging our vehicle. I told Takako, "We're in the Bronx, New York, which is a world renowned crime center, there are not a lot of nice people around here . . . Don't open the door for anyone while I'm gone . . ."

Takako looked scared, but she smiled and said, "Ok." and I went inside and got our shipment delivered.

I had to come back outside to get some paperwork that pertained to our shipment and I noticed that Takako looked totally petrified.

"Did you just tell someone to bring your little Black bag to you?"

"No," I answered!

"Well someone just came to the truck and said that you said for them to bring your little Black bag to you, so I gave it to them," she said.

I was totally pissed.

"Woman, I thought that I just told you not to talk to anyone while I was gone . . . That bag had a $200.00 set of hair clippers and my tooth brush and everything in it!"

She held her head down and with the expression of a guilty two year old child, she said . . . "I'm sorry that I didn't listen to you . . ."

I told her, "This isn't some small town in Japan, it's really dangerous around here, so don't talk to anybody else or let anyone in the truck with you and the children."

"Ok, she said . . ." As she scanned the area suspiciously.

When I went back inside and told the receiver what had happened he got totally pissed.

He was like, "Oh my fucking God, where are you from guy?"

"Memphis," I answered.

"Well this isn't Memphis, you had better watch your ass around here . . . You see those missing cobblestones in the street," he yelled!

"Drug addicts dug them up to sell for drug money!"

"Oh my God," I said, "They could have stabbed my wife and children!"

"Nope, they don't have guns and knives because you can trade them for cash at the pawn shop," he said!

I had never heard of anything like this before, so I told him, "Listen man, get that shit off of my truck and I'm getting out of here . . ."

"You don't have to be scared," he said . . . "You just have to be careful and watch your ass."

On another occasion, while I was out on the road and she was at home with the children, she said that a strange Black lady had come over to the house and asked to use the phone, so this idiot let her in and she roamed all over the house taking things and after she had taken everything that she could carry, she left.

When I called home to check on how everyone was doing, she told me the story . . . I was totally livid.

I had to tell this grown ass woman again, "Don't let strangers in the house . . . You should know that," I yelled!

I was totally pissed, because we had been through several rounds of this kind of kindergarten type stupid ass bullshit and given that women live and breathe to keep up drama, I thought that she was trying to piss me off for some reason.

In a soft, guilty voice, almost crying, she muttered, "I'm sorry, I won't do it again . . ." Then she started complaining that she didn't want to live in America anymore, she said that she wanted to go home to Japan where it was much safer for her and the children and she said that she wanted to raise the children by herself.

I thought that she was just angry because I had yelled at her, so I apologized to her for yelling . . . Because I'm not a screamer and as far as I'm concerned, such behavior is exclusively reserved for bitches, and I never thought about it again.

Then this bitch pulled something that brought an end to the entire fucking world!

I was at home one day and my grandfather got out of the bed and went to the restroom, I was walking behind him, headed to another area of the house and he was so weak that he bumped into the dining room table and his pajamas rubbed against his leg to reveal a skeletal figure, I grabbed him and he was made of absolutely nothing, he had literally been starved to death . . . I instantly had tears in my eyes to the point that I was blinded.

"Why haven't you been eating," I asked him?!

He mumbled something unintelligible back to me and went into the restroom . . . he couldn't talk either.

I immediately asked my wife, "Why haven't you been feeding him?!"

Again, looking like a guilty kindergartener, she replied, "He won't eat anything that I cook, he refuses everything that I try to give him . . . Plus, he peed on me."

Unlike my impudent sister, I had never yelled at my grandfather in my entire life, however, being scared to death that I'd lose him, I went back to my grandfather's room and I yelled at him, "Why haven't you been eating?!"

He started waving both of his hands at me for me to calm down . . . "My mouth has been hurting me," he said finally.

"Why didn't you say something so I could have got you to a doctor," I asked, now completely blinded with tears?

"You were too busy working to take care of your family . . . I didn't want to bother you," he told me.

I could have fainted . . . "I have never been too busy to take care of my own grandfather," I told him.

I was totally dumbfounded, how in the hell could something like this have happened with my wife living in the house with him and his sister, who generally cooked for him, living right next door. I never even remotely dreamed of the possibility of something like this happening.

My grandfather was hospitalized and within two weeks, the greatest master that I had ever had in my entire life had died while I was in a hotel room recovering from a nightmare surgery on a side impacted wisdom tooth that had to have all of the bone cut away from around it and then be cut in three pieces and removed piece by piece and then it had to be dug out because part of the tooth had a curved root on it . . .

I was on a liquid diet for a week.

When I called home from the hotel that I had checked into to get some rest, I found out that my grandfather had died, I could feel no pain . . . I had never been one to turn to alcohol as a solution for any of my problems, but I started drinking beer right after a freshly removed side impacted tooth to make me feel better.

My wife told me that my grandfather had in fact died from Cancer, that's why he had lost so much weight, not because she had starved him . . . For decades on end, my grandfather had had a large growth on his lower jaw and he had always said that it was because of an accident that he had when he was a teenager, but the doctors said that it had in fact been a cancer that had laid dormant while he had his strength, but when he became weak, it rose up on him and killed him.

Just to show you that there's nothing like family, none of the women in my family had ever given a shit about the fate of my grandfather's property or appreciated all of the forty plus years of twenty hours per day work that he had done for the family business, Culpepper's Chicken Shack, one single bit, beyond bragging rights of being a member of the Culpepper Family . . . However, upon his death, there was absolutely no hesitation when it came to stealing everything that he had worked for in life.

His loathsome sister's even more loathsome daughter came down from Chicago and wrote a fake will for him, signed with an X that people sign when they are not at their full mind or a document has been forged, that had all kinds of inconsistencies in it, such as distribution of land and houses that he no longer owned complete with a funeral obituary that made mention of Masonic rites and ceremonies when granddaddy hadn't been a Mason in more than thirty years, which is why he had a missing finger.

This rotten, thieving, lowlife bitch put the notification of the will in some totally obscure newspaper that no one even knew existed . . . And then she had the nerve to get in my face and tell me that I make plenty of money as a truck driver so I had absolutely no need to inherit any of my grandfather's property . . . That was important because it had long been known that I was to be the sole inheritor of his entire estate, which these people, along with my sister, had long claimed not to care about.

I was ready to strangle this rotten whore to death with piano wire, but these thieves had done nothing but scheme and try to figure out how to rob people their whole lives . . .

They were betting heavily that I would rather let all of the property that they had stolen from my grandfather go than kill some of these son of a bitches and have legal problems while my children were toddlers.

I thought the whole thing through and one of the big legal complications was that, I was a grandchild who did not have a copy of my grandfather's will and my mother, whom was on the run from the state for living just like these other assholes from Chicago, was the next legal heir before me and since my mother was one of the most loathsome people that I had ever known, I decided that I would rather forfeit what was supposed to have been mines and move to Japan with my wife rather than have any contact with my mother, whom no one knew the whereabouts of anyway.

While all of this commotion was going on, my wife had been on the phone with her father and had secured the funds for her and the children to move to Japan, which we had long planned anyway. So by January of 1996, less than five months later, she and the children were living in the land of the rising sun and I was to come over and join them as soon as they found a place for us to live and got settled in.

As for me, immediately following the tragic loss of my grandfather I spent about six months having strange dreams of my grandfather in which he would come home from work with some groceries, as he always did, and he would be talking to me but I couldn't hear what he was saying and when I would reach for him he'd instantly disappear and I would wake up crying uncontrollably and no matter how many times I had this recurring dream or how close I let him get to me before I leapt at him and tried to grab him, he would disappear and I would again wake up crying uncontrollably.

My grandfather was nothing short of a God to me, he had passed me a tremendous amount of Intrinsic Law and made sure that I completely understood it for the benefit of future generations and he could go right over my head in an instant and spring something on me that took years to fully comprehend.

For example, one time I had just got a new trucking job and my grandfather put on some casual dinner clothes and told me, "Take me to the man that you work for, we are going out to lunch together."

"Yes Sir," I answered.

We drove down to the extremely trashy trucking company that I worked at and I got out of the pickup and went in and saw the recruiter, a man named, Mr. Shelton, who was always pretty easy to communicate with.

I told him, "Mr. Shelton, my grandfather told me that he wanted me to bring him to the man that I worked for so that we could have lunch together."

Mr. Shelton looked around the office, everyone seemed to be pretty busy, so he said . . .

"Ok, son, I'll go to lunch with you and your grandad."

We all got into Mr. Shelton's car and went to The Piccadilly Restaurant. On the way to the restaurant, my grandfather started lecturing me.

"Son, I want you to take good care of this man's equipment . . . He has given you a huge amount of responsibility and he is trusting you with more than $100,000.00 worth of his equipment, so be sure that you take good care of it, along with a few more pointers."

"Yes Sir," I told him. "I'll be sure to take care of the equipment."

We finally arrived at the restaurant and had lunch and came back and got in my pickup truck and went home and I never thought about any of it again beyond following my grandfather's instructions to the letter as always. It was years later, when I was again meditating on all that my grandfather had told me that I realized that Mr. Shelton had took care of me for years and I had worked with him at at least three different trucking companies because of the simple trip to a restaurant with my grandfather that I never thought anything about . . .

It only made me think that I had to do so much more extremely deep meditation to attempt to comprehend all that my grandfather had said and done for me.

SEXCAPADES

AFTER THE TREMENDOUS stress of having lost both my grandfather and inheritance, I was in a deep depression for quite some time, all that I did was work, hang out at trashy trucker bars and hang out with trashy whores on the back rows of even trashier truck stops.

While I was supposed to be sending money home to support my family and saving up money to go and join my family in Japan, it was in fact everything that I could do to get through the days after experiencing that high a level of anxiety and hideousness.

West Memphis, Arkansas became my second home for years on end and I did everything there from truckin' and fuckin' to scaring the shit out of crazy, spaced out crack whores by revving my engine and pretending to chase them around the parking lot of the truck stops with my big truck when they made me mad.

Some of the shit that I experienced between there and a club called The 6 that I frequented when I was in town was shit that I had long planned to write a book called Ho' Tales and Mo' Tales about.

Given that I had been raised and mentored by Pimps since I was a toddler on the track where my family had a bar-b-que restaurant for decades, as well as random masters that I had encountered all over the country, I had nothing less than a gift with hookers and I could get them to go anywhere and do anything and while other people got demoralized and ripped off by prostitutes, I rarely got ripped off and I always had a super-great time with them, whether I was riding their grimy ass, Pimping on them, had them Pimping on me, whether I was engaging in fun and games with hookers or whether I was trying to convince them to get out of whoredom to save their own lives, I always had a barrel of fun with the girls and when I was lucky, I even ran across an old high ranking true master Pimp and was fortunate enough to receive a good Pimpnological lecture.

Since I was trained by true master Pimps my whole life, I didn't have any game and when I did manage to put some good game over on a whore, it was always a huge laugh for me and my friends who were Macks.

For example, one time in West Memphis I ran into one of my favorite wildcat whores and I told her that I wanted to look at her pussy while she was sucking my dick, so, being the quintessential contortionist she curled up in the perfect position and we had a wonderful experience together.

Since we had known each other for years on end and she was feeling a bit relaxed that day . . . she said, "Don't worry, you can pay me $50.00 after we do our thing . . ."

We did the doo and then we climbed back up front into the cab of the truck, she let down the windows and I gave her two twenties and a ten . . . It was windy that day in West Memphis and there were cool, heavy gusts of wind sporadically blowing through the truck that felt like Heaven on Earth . . . After a few minutes of sitting there a really strong gust of wind hit us and blew the cash right out of her hand.

That was unexpected, we both looked at each other like a couple of Hispanics who had just seen Jesus on a piece of toast . . . Then she freaked out and started crying.

"My God, I needed that money, I worked so hard for that money," she lamented . . .

I told her, "It's alright baby, it's out there somewhere, it couldn't have gone that far . . ."

She bolted out of the truck and went looking around the parking lot for the cash . . . After she had been out there for about 15 minutes, I got out of the truck to try to help her . . .

She had wandered pretty far away from the truck looking for her hard earned money and as I started searching, first I looked under the truck . . . Nothing there. Then I walked around the truck . . . Still nothing. Then I looked between the frame of the truck and the fuel tank on the passenger side and there were two twenties and a ten laying in the crease between the fuel tank and frame. I picked up the money, put it in my pocket, walked back around the truck and got back in.

After a few minutes, she came back worn out, tired and depressed . . . "I can't believe that I can't find that money anywhere, what am I gonna do?"

"Well, since you're a pretty nice girl I can go in to the ATM and get another $50.00 and we can do another date and you'll have your $50.00 back and you'll still have just as much pussy as you had when you showed up," I said smiling.

"Awww, that's so sweet, would you do that for me," she asked?

"I would do that for you," I replied with a big chicken shit smile. So we cruised across the street to the truck stop, I walked in to the ATM and stood there for a few minutes, then I walked back out to the truck and gave her that same $50.00 and I hit the pussy again and both of our lives were again filled with laughter.

I have long heard that there are people who can count money in pitch darkness without see it, and given that I have had a lifetime of experience with hookers, I eventually experienced it.

I was parked at a rest area in Texarkana when Carla the crazy crack whore came over to my truck. I was pretty starved for pussy, so I decided that I would have a taste.

She climbs up on the truck and I invited her back into my office and she asks me how much I want to spend, I countered by asking her for a bit of legally required indecent exposure first and she pulls out her deflated tit and swears up and down that she's not a cop, which progresses us to the point where we can talk trashy, sex trade business.

I told her, "Baby, I have $82.00, but I have to eat, so I am only able to spend $40.00."

"What do you want," she asked?

"Half and half," I answered.

"I usually get more than $40.00 for half and half, are you sure that you can't do better than that?"

"I can go $42.00 and I have some change in my change jar."

"Ok, I don't usually work like that, but I won't take everything that you've got . . ."

"Thank You," I told her.

I gave her $42.00 and about $3.00 in change, we rolled in the hay and when she left I was just sitting there relaxing . . . After about thirty minutes when I finally checked my pockets, I only had $2.00 left . . .

Like the average idiot, thinking that it was just my imagination or that I had somehow misplaced my cash, when I eventually figured out that this trashy little rat, who was actually sitting on the far end of the bunk from me and never came down on my end, somehow, reached around behind me, separated the four twenties from the two ones and got in the wind before I could think about catching her.

The bitch got me, but like she said, she didn't take everything that I had.

I knew a trashy little nymphomaniac in Knoxville who called herself Peppermint Patty, as far as I knew, Patty had never done anything in her life but whore and she swore that all five or six of her sisters were whores too, however, that happens.

Patty was a wonderful ride and if you were a trashy trucker, she could give you a run for your money. She had a vagina that was a living miracle and she was so freaky that if you had an erection and she saw cum in the head of the condom, she would bite the condom open and damn near suck your insides out.

Since I'm a social animal and a highly capable and experienced Pimpnological inquisitor who loves solving Pimpnological problems, over the years I have had people make some very rare and interesting confessions to me.

Confessions of the kind that people would comparatively only normally make to their physician.

I used to hang out and trash around in Nashville at a truck stop right off of Dickerson Pike (The name says it all) which contrary to the determined efforts of the Nashville Police Department continues to be a source of whores and crack and crackwhores, several of whom have been run over and killed while dancing or otherwise strutting their nasty little stuff out on I65 during rush hour.

Though I'd spent years having my trashy fun there and seeing things that would make the Devil say damn, occasionally I also got to help people that were desperately in need of Pimpnological solutions.

For example, I had this coworker who was absolutely petrified of spending money because his domineering wife would firmly chastise him. One day, we found ourselves laid over until we got loaded the next day and I suggested that we go to a nearby seafood restaurant.

"Seafood Restaurant," he repeated, nearly trembling. "That sounds expensive, I can't spend any money out here or my wife will kill me."

"Don't worry guy," I told him. "It's all on me . . . So you won't have any explaining to do."

Though he was quite literally afraid for his life, I finally coaxed him into going, just to keep me company.

We arrived at a pretty decent seafood restaurant and we got seated and ordered . . . He was very nervously checking his watch every few minutes.

I finally asked him, "Are you ok guy?"

"My wife usually calls me at about this time of day to see what I'm doing and if she finds out that I'm out having seafood, she's really going to get me."

As if it were an omen, his phone started ringing.

"Oh my God, my phone is ringing, it's her . . . What am I going to do," he said in a panic?

"Answer it, and tell her that one of your coworkers took you out to dinner," I told him.

He mustered the nerve to answer the call from his lady and her first question was, what is that music playing in the background, where are you at, and he totally fucking freaked?

"Oh my God," he said silently, as if he was about to release a silent scream . . . "She's asking about the background music, what am I going to tell her," he said in a panic?

"Tell her that you are in Hell right now," I told him.

"What," he said as high eyes bucked?!

"I can't tell her that."

"Trust me, every woman in this world wants to know that her man is in Hell," I told him . . ."Tell her that you are in Hell and she will burst out laughing."

With his voice nearly tremoring, he finally told her, "I'm in Hell right now," as he swallowed hard.

"I can't believe it, she's giggling," he told me as his hand covered the phone.

Boy was he living on the edge that night . . .

I hope that she didn't kick his ass too bad when he finally rotated back in . . .

I have always said that abused husbands are the silent victims.

On another occasion when I was passing through Nashville, I wound up talking to this twenty something year old kid who was also trucking while we were having lunch. During our conversational rambling, I happened to mention to him that I wrote books about the factors that drive people to live self-destructive lifestyles.

"How did you learn to do that," he asked?

"I grew up during an era when pandering and prostitution were epidemic in this country and since I was highly respectful to masters on the street I was often chosen as one of their disciples and received countless lectures and hands-on pinpoint precise training from them," I told him.

After delving off into a lengthy and quite in-depth lecture on the Pimping driven by the random questions that he continued to drill me with, the young man told me . . .

"Man, I've never told anyone this before, but my sister is actually a prostitute . . ."

I smiled, "Ok," I told him.

"I never would have told you that, but I was listening to what you were saying about whores being counter-reactionary extremists who have their subconscious anxieties running their lives and whores being like pinballs that bounce back and forth between predators and panderers until they eventually wind up in the gutter," he said. "That kind of caught my interest."

"I kept hearing rumors that my sister was out on the track until I finally went down to the track to see if she was down there and my sister was out on the track," he told me distraughtly.

"I caught her and told her that, no sister of mine is gonna be a whore and if she didn't get off of the track right now I would disown her . . ."

"Whoa, whoa, whoa, hold it right there," I told him.

"That's the worst thing that you could have possibly done . . ."

"I didn't know what else to do," he told me.

"Now, I don't know your sister's particular situation, but in many cases, wide open fast track whores are drama junkies and it's like cocaine, you're not going to get a coke head off of coke by feeding more of it to them and the same is true of drama junkies, if a woman is hooked on drama, you're not going to reel her back in by creating the drama of giving her an anxiety inducing ultimatum . . ."

"That makes sense," he conceded.

"Many masters will say, let them buck until they get the wild or anxiety out of their system, because they know that it takes such a tremendous amount of anxiety to propel a woman to wide open fast track whoring that once they start to expend that energy, they will soon run out of anxiety or negative energy and revert back to a normal mode of living."

"However, if you want your sister back, I need to know, does your family still have contact with her?"

He was like, "Yeah, we hear from her on holidays . . ."

"Good, that means that she's not strung that far out on anxiety and she is not beyond your family's reach."

"Let me ask you another diagnostic question, how many children were in your family?"

"About eight." he said.

I smiled real big . . . "Eight sounds great," I told him . . . "This gets us closer to an accurate diagnosis of severe anxiety."

"Eight children leaves a lot of room for the generation of tremendous anxiety, for example, without noticing, every time that your family had chicken for dinner, someone could have got the wing every time and over the years it just ate at them until they finally blew up or felt completely left out."

"You know, one time when I was talking to her, she got mad and yelled, none of y'all ever gave a damn about me . . . I didn't know what the hell she was talking about!"

"Uh huh, try this," I told him . . . "The next time that your family hears from her on the holidays, tell her that you all miss her and you all are praying for her everyday . . . As she bounces back and forth and continues to turn to people in desperation, if your family is in the mix, without knowing, she will eventually turn to her family in desperation too . . ."

"As for her Pimp, if she is surviving his Pimping, there is no real need to worry about him . . . Contrary to popular belief, no woman is a whore for life, Pimps and prostitutes are invariably highly relationship dysfunctional individuals and the omen of brutal fast track whore-Pimps is that all too often they are murdered, incarcerated or just plain dumped by their women and the harder that a cat tries to Pimp on a whore the harder that that whore is going to blow back when she finally blows back on him," I told him . . . then I had to get in the wind.

When I was going through the considerable motions of trying to organize the Mount Everest of personal notes that I had written and had to sort through to turn the message fragments for my book Pimps: The Raw Truth into an intelligible wealth of information, I spent a lot of time at Kinkos Copy Shop printing up and reviewing manuscripts.

One of the places that I did a considerable amount of this highly meticulous work was Cedar Rapids, Iowa, which is a quirky little town with a comparatively high suicide rate, links to the space program and a steady flow of loathsome ghetto trash from Chicago all of which are factors that come together to yield a culture of inadvertent prejudice.

One of the pretty little girls who had a full schedule at Kinkos and always seemed to be working when I went there, was obviously somehow reading my manuscripts, because after a while, though she remained courteous, when she would take my manuscript back to the copier to print it, she would hold it with the tips of her fingers like it was the tail of a highly grotesque, dead, mildewed rat . . . Which I got a laugh out of, because I really didn't care if she liked the project or not, it was only important to me that she printed it so that I could move forward with the process of publishing it.

One day when I came in, she was exceptionally perky and friendly, which immediately made me suspicious, because I know all too well that all women are mean people and when they are showing their teeth they are either only pretending to be nice or they are up to something . . .

This one was up to something.

My haughty little White friend needed some vital information from what she clearly perceived as a total scumbag, so she felt that she had to put on her best smile . . .

I notice that this time she was holding my manuscript like it was an actual printing job as opposed to a dead rodent and while it was printing, she looked around to see that no one was near us and then she leaned in close to me and said under her voice . . .

"I need to ask you something."

Showing my teeth, "Fire away," I answered.

"There is a guy that comes in here that I absolutely cannot make sense of, he's not kind and even tempered like you . . . He's very different, one day he will come in and be very nice to me, then he'll come in and be very rude to me, then he'll bring me a present . . . I absolutely can't make any sense of it."

I told her, "He wants you and he's trying out different tactics on you to see what you'll go for."

Appalled, her expression soured, "Well that's totally not the way to catch me. However, it does make sense . . . Thanks," she said . . . Then she handed me my manuscript and I left.

On another occasion, I was in Toronto, Ontario having a few beers and some seafood at this scuzzy little restaurant that had great seafood and a sky high employee turnover rate; which is a clear sign that someone is being exploited. And just like always, I show up and there's a brand new female employee running the bar . . . Only this one is much meaner than any of the others that I have encountered.

As she talked to what was clearly a regular customer at the place, she started bitching about how she really hates it when people try to help her understand things at a new job, like they think that she's stupid or something . . . Then she starts bitching about how she's tired of her parents always trying to help her out, because she's a grown woman who can do things herself.

Then she starts bitching about how tired she is of one of her children's fathers trying to get back with her. Then she starts bitching about how pissed off she is about her uterus having grown back after she had it lasered so that she couldn't have any more children and how she wound up having to have an abortion because of it.

Then I noticed that every time that she sold a drink, she put the bottle caps in a pile. When someone asked her why she was keeping all of those bottle caps, she completely exploded and yelled at the poor slob who was unfortunate enough to have asked the question that, "It's how I make good and goddamn sure that I'm not getting cheated at the end of the night . . . When my shift is over, there's no fucking ifs and ands or buts about how many beers I've sold or how much these damn people owe me and there's no debates about me having stolen or tried to cheat them out of anything . . . I just count up my bottle caps and everything comes out even!!!"

As I observed her as I sat there and casually had a drink, in my mind this woman had progressed from a bitch to a whore to a rotten whore in the span of two minutes flat. She had been completely made in the span of 120 seconds.

Then she went outside on the patio to have a cigarette and I told the guy sitting next to me that this woman had clearly been a prostitute before.

He looks over at me and says, "Don't say that, because that guy over there is going to go right out there and tell her everything that you said."

"Oh," I said . . . "He must be a taxi driver."

"How did you know that," he answered?

Before he could get the words out of his mouth, trying to score points with this bitch, the other guy had already jumped off of his stool and run out there and told her everything. She instantly looks totally angry and she bolts back in the door and comes over to me and rudely asks, "Is there anything else that I can get for you?!"

As if it's time to close out my ticket.

"Another beer please, thank you," I answered.

Then, just to fuck with her, I asked her if there were any prostitutes around there.

The guy next to me cringed, he couldn't believe that I had went there after she already knew that I had made her as a whore.

"There aren't any whores around here, all of the whores hang out around Market Street."

"What are you looking for a whore," she asked me?

"Not particularly, I'm just interested," I answered.

Then she tells me that she knows all about the whores and she used to work as a rehab therapist for prostitutes.

"How do you qualify for the that," I asked her?

She gave me a glaring look.

"I see," I answered.

Naturally being confrontational, she said, "I know that you think that you're smart and you know a lot about hookers, but you don't know shit about prostitutes."

"How do you figure that," I asked her?

"What do you think that you are, some kind of Pimp," she yells at me!

"You don't know shit about Pimping!"

Then, raising my voice slightly, I told her, "I clearly know enough to have made your ass, didn't I?!"

"That still don't make you no Pimp!"

Then I yelled at her, "Bitch, as a matter of fact I'm a motherfucking master Pimp from Memphis, Tennessee, which is one of the biggest Pimpnological centers in the fucking world that breeds, trains and dispatches Pimps all over North America!"

The bitch looked at me like I had just threatened her life.

I also had Pimpnological solutions for little people.

I can recall the son of a bona fide Mack who could pull pussy out of thin air. Most Macks had game, however, this Mack had charisma and real live Mack tactics, until he played himself and lost everything . . . Which is why I'm not a big fan of playing on people.

Anyway, me and Mackilicious had been running buddies for years, he knew me from back in the days when I had just been released from being an elder-train-ee, trainee, which is the trainee of an elder trainee and the totally uncontested head of the youth club in my region in a religious organization where I worked and studied both etymology and The Holy Bible on a strict, set schedule of twenty hours per day for two and a half years, which combined with years of Pimpnological training can yield disciples who are far beyond insanely determined.

This guy had two sons and I had two daughters who often played together until my wife started to feel that the boys played too rough and were too wild and undisciplined to play with our very lady like daughters, especially after one of the girls showed up with ballpoint pen marks around her eyes.

Much later, after my girls had been moved to Japan to assure that they were raised in a decent environment with proper parents and grandparents, I still maintained contact with the Mack and his family and kept them updated on my intercontinental exploits in Japan.

The Mack's sons had spent a tremendous amount of time with the Mack and I when I was in the country and they knew all too well that I relentlessly studied solutions to all kinds of problems and never got into anything that even remotely resembled trouble.

Once, I happened to breeze back into town and I noticed that one of the Mack's junior high school aged sons was looking depressed . . . I asked him how he was doing, why he seemed depressed and if everything was ok at school?

He told me that things in fact weren't going so well at school, so I asked him what was happening at school to get him down, we were a quite lively bunch when I was a junior high school student.

He revealed that someone at school was bullying him because since his family lived on a strict non-hormonal diet, he wasn't nearly as big as the other children who had been raised on the hormones, steroids and emulsifiers that largely underlie North American epidemic obesity and makes the average North American boy look like a linebacker and the average North American girl completely indistinguishable from a full-figured, voluptuous, sexually active adult.

This kid was a beautiful little boy and all that a Pimp really wanted in this life . . . A young, highly capable disciple.

"Who is this character," I asked him? . . .

"He is a kid that arrived at our school as a result of having been suspended from so many other schools that our school is the only school that he can go to before he is suspended from being able to go to school in the entire state.

"Who else is this person bullying," I asked him?

"It can't just be you . . ."

"He also likes to feel on girls, he calls himself a Pimp," he told me.

I just shook my head in disapproval, I had to tell him, "Listen baby, your friend sounds really confused and misguided to me . . . Pimps are not interested in feeling on girls, all that Pimps want to feel on is cash money. Pimps get paid from other people wanting to feel on girls, ya dig."

"Your guy might aspire to be a little player or Mack or something but feeling on girls is absolutely not Pimping, so we can eliminate that . . ." He still looked depressed.

"This is the law baby, in this life, things go like they come . . . If things come to you quickly, you'll lose them quickly, if someone has fouled to you, they will foul away from you . . . if this cat came to you on a suspension, he will be suspended away from you."

"Here's a solution to your problem, in a militant situation, you always want to spot your opponent first, in this particular case, this individual is going to screw up and be completely suspended out of the entire school system . . . All that he needs is just a little time."

As I tried to get my philosophy on staying out of shit; which is that "The best way to stay out of shit is to stay out of shit and it works," across to this kid! I told him, "Keep your eyes open, always spot this cat first and completely avoid him . . . Let him pass you, and before you know it, you'll never see him again in this life."

After receiving a practical solution, he felt much better . . . I blew town and about two weeks later I happened to rotate back and I made it a point to go and see him, just in case he needed further guidance.

When I saw him again he looked like he was on top of the world.

"How's your little buddy doing," I asked him?

"Oh he's gone, we won't be seeing him again," he laughed.

"What did he wind up doing?"

"He felt on some girl and she tried to fight him, he beat her up and school officials took him away," he said with a triumphant smile.

"Excellent," I told him . . . "You're completely unscathed and your problem is gone for life!"

His ghetto parents wanted him to fight this kid, which was absolute last resort insanity.

He was so happy to be through with that problem that he didn't know what to do and since no one had even remotely had a solution for him except a Pimp, he was sitting at the kitchen table tossing dice.

He definitely aspired to be a hustler at that point, however, in reality, he clearly had a pretty big misconception about how a true master Pimp calculates, thinks and works to solve problems. In reality, true master Pimping is not a hustle, it's intrinsic law and it requires a tremendous amount of meditation, guidance and hands-on training to avoid it becoming self-detrimental.

The world being the zoo that it is, instead of his parents thanking me for helping and being happy that their son was doing and feeling much better . . . These two ghettofied idiots chose to banish me from their family, separate from each other and the Mack wound up playing himself and becoming a homeless drug addict.

However, Macks weren't always tragic, I also knew super-fun Macks like Cole as well.

Cole was a commercial driver like myself, however, the difference between us, was that, while I could pull Pimp paying whores out of thin air, Cole could pull pussy and several months of literally any bitches whole paycheck out of thin air. And unlike Cole, I worked solely to support my family, while Cole worked solely to accommodate his game.

Cole was a Mega-Mack who had so much game that he was juggling bitches like Bozo The Clown . . . I can remember one chick in particular, she was a big, thick, fine goddess of a twenty something year old White woman who had just hired onto a container hauling operation that we were all working at at the time when I first met Cole.

When this big, thick, fine, super-star ass White bitch walked across the parking lot it was always a major event that would literally stop traffic, people were watching this bitch like she was going to steal something.

And when a bunch of guys gathered around and tried to come up with some tactics to try to catch her . . . Cole told everyone that they could absolutely and completely forget about the White woman, she was his and he would have her within two weeks . . .

All of the guys, except me, laughed in Cole's face, even though I had an angelic Asian wife at home, I wanted the big, juicy White bitch too, but I didn't laugh at Cole because I had grown up and been trained by Macks and Pimps my whole life and I knew all too well that when it came to women, they were highly capable of performing miracles that a woman didn't know that she didn't even remotely have a choice in.

Right on schedule, within a week Cole had the White woman's phone number and by the next week he had her eating out of his hand. After a few months she quit the company and moved to Nashville where she had got a new job as an airline stewardess and Cole regularly got loads to Nashville so that he could see her in between playing on other women.

The Mackin' had triumphed again, wonderful for him, but by far, nothing new to me.

Cole's game was extremely strong, but sometimes I had to avoid him and be cautious of his game, so that it didn't get me taken out of this life.

For example, one year we had a company Christmas Party at another outfit that we worked at together and on the night of the Christmas Party, I went to West Memphis, Arkansas and invited some crack whores that I knew to the Christmas Party, but nobody that I wanted to go to the party with wanted to go with me . . . Apparently, celebrating Christmas is against crack whore's religion.

I walk in the door and received greetings from all of my trashy trucker friends and coworkers. As I started to dig into the culinary accommodations and socialize with a White driver that I often socialized with . . . I told him, "I just went over to West Memphis to try to get some of the whores to come to the Christmas Party with me."

Under his voice, he said that he had thought about doing the same thing, but he was scared that someone might recognize one of the girls as he looked around conspicuously trying to be sure that no one else was listening . . .

I told him that I wouldn't have gave a fuck who recognized my crack whore date, it would have just been some more shit for us to laugh about later.

After I got some chow, I scanned the room for a place to sit. There were open seats on either side of a beautiful White woman wearing an absolutely stunning sequin jacket. I almost fainted, no doubt, the boss's wife.

As a Pimp, I love clothes more than any woman and I personally knew of Macks who were so good at shopping for women that women who had no color coordination and couldn't pick out anything that they thought looked good on them themselves, would actually pay these cats cash money to go shop for them whenever they needed event level clothing.

I walked over and sat next to her and I told her that, "I couldn't help noticing your beautiful red, White and blue sequin jacket. It's absolutely stunning, where on Earth did you find it, I know that you didn't get it around here?"

"No darling, I got it in Atlanta for a mere $12,000.00," she retorted.

"Scrumptious," I answered.

Then Cole, The Mega-Mack, walks in with a date and everybody looks over to see what this guy is up to . . .

Perhaps a sinister ploy to take down the boss's wife?

You never really knew with this guy.

The Mack eventually walks over toward me, so I greet him . . .

"Cole, my man, what's happening?!"

He smiled real big and sat next to me, "I'll tell you what's happen Pimpin', Merry Christmas, that's what's happening . . ."

Then he started pointing out women.

"You see that one over there," he asked me?

"Uh huh," I answer him.

"That's my date," he told me.

"Ok."

"You see that one over there and that one over there and the one that I came in with?"

"Uh huh," I answered him again.

"All four of them are my dates and neither one of them knows it," then he showed me his teeth.

I look over at him and start laughing, then I told him, "Negro, I don't know if I should be sitting next to you."

He looks over and answers, "Why don't you want to sit next to me?"

"Because if some of these bitches get to shooting up in here, I could get caught in the cross-fire . . ."

And we both busted out laughing, then he went off to fuck with somebody else.

A few years later, I encountered Cole at yet a third outfit that we mysteriously wound up working at together, he was still up to his same old games and tricks.

At this outfit, there was a White woman who was so mean that we called her Wicked Wanita . . . and she was my dispatcher, so I talked to her everyday . . . and I nicknamed her Wanda Woman.

She kept hounding me about it being a miracle that I was able to stay married with my wife living in another country and she eventually starts drilling me inside out about not having a woman in the U.S. . . .

I told her that I only catch whores and intellectuals, never ordinary women . . . So she tries to analyze me and give me some dating advice, like buying a pickup truck and hanging out at the Walmart in West Memphis, Arkansas where she lived . . .

I told her that the back row of a trashy truck stop was really more my scene . . . Then she told me, maybe you talk to whores so much that without realizing it you are talking to ordinary women like they're whores and it is offending them . . ..

I told her that I'm really not a rude person and my luck with women is just an omen of possessing extreme amounts of ominous Pimp energy.

Then Wanita finally came out and asked me to go out on a date.

I had to turn Wanita down, because I am absolutely not into fool acting women and though, unlike strong, totally independent Black women who take tremendous pride in acting totally unparalleled idiots, she was a White woman who was capable of pretending to have sensibility, but I knew that Wanita could act an absolute and complete idiot with little to no provocation because as one of her drivers I talked to her on the phone several times a day.

"Let's go out sometimes," she told me.

"I can't Wanita," I told her.

"Why not," she asked me, her wicked temper already starting to become heated.

"Because you're too damn mean," I told her! . . .

Plus, she had an ass that looked like a deflated basketball . . . And I needed an ass that was big and juicy.

She was totally pissed.

Her flat butt and bad attitude had deterred me, but it apparently had not deterred The Mack.

I was cruising toward the yard one day through the industrial area that our outfit was located in, and I saw The Mack coming towards me driving Wanita's car smiling like he'd just won the freaking lottery.

And I thought to myself, "Oh my God, he's probably taking half of her paycheck like he was doing to so many other women simultaneously."

After seeing this, I decided that when I got to the yard I was going to have some fun with this mean bitch.

I swung into the yard, parked my truck and I ran into the office so that I was breathing heavily.

"Wanita, where are your keys, I need to borrow your car, it's an emergency," I told her breathing heavily.

Being Wicked Wanita, she totally freaks out and starts yelling at me, "I can't give you my car!!!"

"Why not," I asked her?

"Because you're not on my insurance."

"Didn't I just see Cole driving your car?"

"That's different," she yelled at me!!!

"I'll bet that it is, because he's The Mack."

Then I told her, "I was just messing with you Wanita, when I saw Cole driving your car, I just had to come and mess with you."

She blushed and looked really embarrassed.

A few weeks later The Mack totally surprised me in the breakroom.

I walked into the breakroom one day and a total goddess of a White woman saw me and jumped up and ran over to me and gave me a big hug and said, "Hey, Eric . . . How have you been doing, I haven't seen you in ages."

I looked kind of dumbfounded, like an idiot . . .

I was standing there looking at her, trying to figure out exactly who she was.

Then she said, "I'm Cole's wife, the airline stewardess, you don't remember me?"

Then I looked at her a bit closer and it was in fact the big, fine, mega-star ass White woman from the container outfit that we had worked at years ago . . . After all of those guys had laughed in his face, The Mack still had her and he had kept her for years . . . All that really surprised me, was that he had dumped his Black wife that he had when he first caught her and he had actually married her. Macks don't usually do this, they generally cop and blow women every few months or weeks like Pimps.

During my vast travels, I have been fortunate enough to be lectured by some of the most highly capable and experienced intrinsic and Pimpnological masters on the planet and this has yielded some great conclusive capabilities.

If Pimpology is focused on, conjured and studied intensely enough, it can give one the ability to see through literally anything based on an in-depth understanding of people and thing's vibes, silhouettes and behavioral patterns.

What distinguishes a religious Pimpnological master from all others, is that he grasps and relentlessly studies the entirety of religion without fear or prejudice because he realizes that it is all ultimately the same highly refined omni-dimensional gangsterdom that has always ruled the world in its various incarnations.

One extreme master, whose lectures stand out in my memory as being extremely relative in today's highly competitive world, was Master Black Rebel.

Black Rebel was a master Pimp and convicted natural born killer who had fought under the CIA in what he said was a top secret program in which life term inmates were offered the opportunity to gain their freedom from incarceration if they survived being dumped into free fire zones with hopelessly low survival rates as they chased Chinese radar in Cambodia during the Vietnam war.

Black Rebel had bulging eyes that looked like he had repelled into the belly of hell and lived to tell about it. As with many Pimpnological masters, very much including myself, I just happened across him in my travels and recognized his energy and he happened to be in the mood to give me a very lengthy, vital and highly in-depth lecture on the vitality of knowledge, skills, tools and access in one's quest for material success along with some tales of his personal experiences piercing the female subconscious.

However, one could reasonably ask, what is the real world practical utility of such knowledge and capabilities?

An excellent example of the real world utility of Pimpnological insights and capabilities would be that, on an occasion when I was on a bus in South Beach, Florida I was wearing a White hat that bared my grand inquisitor level Pimpnological crest that is on the cover of my master work titled, Pimps: The Raw Truth Grand Inquisitor Level Pimpnological Conclusions and a young man from some part of India started to question me about my hat's symbolism, which was somewhat irritating, given the level of secrecy that surrounds things of Indian origin, but I entertained him.

He had a very specific interest in Pimpnological criminal and behavioral profiling techniques.

A homeless White man who had just exited the bus needed some money so I gave him $20.00 in exchange for a highly exquisite work of artwork that he had just made. Though I thought that it was a grasshopper, he said that it was a dragon and it had been made from toothpicks and blades of grass . . . I thought that it was absolutely beautiful . . .

"Exactly how does criminal profile work," he questioned.

"This for example," I told him, as I held up the rare work of art that I had just purchased . . . "This is the kind of thing that would be made by a person who has an extremely high amount of time on their hands, like a prisoner . . . This would be a person who could make deadly weapons out of simple objects like a spoon or a toothbrush and they would be quite proficient at hiding drugs or weapons in their ass."

The passengers on the bus looked shocked, then some Black lady who rides the bus everyday said that she had once heard him mention that he had been in prison . . .

"There," I told him, "It works like that . . ."

Upon disembarking the bus, I put the piece of art on a high ledge and a Hispanic woman who could not reach it asked me if she could have the work of art and I gave it to her.

Another more basic utility of Pimpnological thinking is avoiding problems with prostitutes.

While I was whoring around North America while my family was in Japan, I happened across a veteran whore named Flash . . . Flash was a nearly 60 year old whore who had never done anything else in her life . . . Flash associated with Pimps, but she had long been a wildcat (a whore without a Pimp).

When I met Flash, she was trying to sell me some damn near 60 year old pussy and since she was a really average looking woman I really wasn't interested.

Flash assured me that she had some good pussy . . . And I reassured her that I really wasn't interested, but I told her that she was free to use my radio to find someone who was interested if she liked.

Flash took me up on my offer and she attempted to do a bit of soliciting, no one else was interested either . . . so Flash sat back, relaxed and managed to talk me into going into the store and buying her some beer . . .

I was laid over and had absolutely nothing to do until the next day, so I went to the store to get her some beer because she said that she had been barred from the store's property because she was a known hooker.

I hop out of my truck, walk across the street to get Flash some beer and when I walk back, I notice that there is a hustler looking Black dude sitting up in my truck and Flash is sitting on his lap . . .

I walked up to my truck, opened the door, climbed up and I was like, "What's up," to the two of them!

I handed Flash her 12 pack of beer, I was feeling generous, so I bought her a 12 pack of beer instead of a six . . . She thanked me, her friend introduced himself as Cochise, a seventies era D.C. Pimp. I introduced myself as Piece of Pimp from Memphis, Tennessee and we all had the 12 pack of beer and kicked it together for hours . . .

When you get a 12 pack of beer, two Pimps and a career hooker together, you have hours of very colorful conversation . . . Everybody in that truck told their whole street life history . . . We really had a great time.

I can remember Flash telling an absolutely hilarious story about buying a Ford Mustang with some good pussy and no credit, proof of employment or work history.

By now sloppy drunk and slurring, she said, "Don't ever let anybody tell you that you can't buy a car with no credit and proof of employment or work history."

"Why shouldn't we let anybody tell us that we can't buy a car with no credit and proof of employment or work history," I asked her?

"Because I've done it goddammit," she said drunkenly!

"A long time ago I financed a car with nothing but some good pussy."

Laughing by now, I asked her, "How on Earth did you buy a car with nothing but some good pussy?"

"Years ago, back in the Eighties, when Ford had those super-fast Mustangs that were so fast that they were killing people, I wanted one . . . So I went to Ford Dealers all over East Tennessee trying to buy one and no one would finance me because I didn't have any credit, proof of employment or work history."

"Then I finally went into this one dealership and talked to a salesman and he talked to me for a few minutes and had me fill out a credit application," and then he said, "Excuse me, I have to go and talk to my manager."

He went over and talked to the manager for a few minutes and then he came back and said, "You're approved!"

"I couldn't believe it! I asked him, how on Earth did you get me approved when I have been turned down by every other dealership in the region?"

"Then the salesman told me," "You don't remember me, but I used to be a detective and I've arrested you several times for trespassing for the purposes of prostitution, so we know that you're good for the money . . . Enjoy your car . . ."

Being drunk, we all just busted out laughing hysterically and started banging on things.

Cochise was a Carolinian who had been a major urban area drug addict Gorilla Pimp, who burned women, broke women's noses and had actually blown his own leg out shooting cocaine and he spent a lot of time going on about how difficult it had been for him to recruit higher grades of pussy, like university students, which made it clear that he had been so street that he had been minimally tactical and highly abusive.

However, since I don't believe in human misery, I never ever resorted to such Gorilla tactics and I was always chastened against them by my Pimpnological masters, right from the beginning of my discipleship when I was eleven and as far as I am concerned, they are absolutely and completely unnecessary and an excellent example of this is a club that I used to frequent called The 6, which was an average dance bar that was a hot whore recruiting spot that attracted a lot of college students and a few Pimps . . .

In hindsight, I think to myself that, had more Pimps known how easy it was to sit up and recruit lovely young women at The 6, it might have been covered up with Pimps . . . which in the grand scheme of things would have ultimately caused it to be trashed out and shut down by the dumb asses among Pimps themselves.

However, one group of ho catchers that it wasn't slowing down were drug addicts . . . I can't count how many times I'd seen guys parade in there, find a couple of absolutely beautiful full figured college girls and smoke them down until they looked like something from The Faces of Death Documentary.

Among several girls who were turned out and recruited by freaks, junkies and Pimps, I can recall one girl in particular that I'd known for years.

She would often appear and disappear and reappear and disappear again and nobody really asked where she was or what she was doing when she was in a phase of absenteeism.

I didn't find out until she showed up one night and offered to give me a really good blow job if I would let her sleep in my truck, that when we didn't see her she had actually been bouncing in and out of drug rehab programs.

"Sleep in my truck," I told her, "You can live in my truck and ride all over the country with me as long as we don't have to be scouring the country looking for crack houses . . ."

"No, no, no, baby, it's nothing like that . . . I don't need to live with you . . . I just need a place to sleep for the night . . ."

"Ok baby, I'll be here," I told her . . . assured that I had a good head job secured for the night.

However, as luck would have it, if it's not my wife or a real live prostitute, I almost always miss out . . . I'm great at whoring, but absolutely horrible at dating.

We actually got all kinds down at The 6 and occasionally we got some characters that could be pretty hard to get a make on.

For example, one night I was sitting in the club staring out of the window and I saw two Black guys sitting in a Cadillac across the street, one of the them had a hairdo as big as that bass player from Earth, Wind and Fire.

I actually thought that they were a couple of faggots at first . . . It turns out that they were a couple of Pimps who were getting weeded up before they came in and scoped out the place and ultimately left and never came back because it was a slow night and they didn't see any quick action.

However, there were other times when who was riding in a particular car was far more obvious . . . At least to me . . . And on the particular night that I had some guaranteed head in the bag, it was just my luck that a Cadillac with gold rims and a vomit pink and gold glitter paint job pulls up with a car load of negros that were so greasy that they looked like they had each washed their face with a bucket of fried chicken.

Completely Mortified, all that I could think was, "Oh my God, my pussy!!!"

They all piled out of their high profile car, piled into the club, they walked over to the dance side of the bar, no apparently easy pickings over there, then they came over on the quiet side of the bar where I was sitting, they scanned the room and looked right past me like I didn't exist and just like a group of synchronized dancers they all focused right in on my piece of action for the night.

They walked over to this bitch, talked to her for less than five minutes, she got up, went over to the other side of the bar with them and I'm just sitting there sighing over my shitty luck, because I'm knowing damn well that I have absolutely nothing in this world that will trump a car load of greaseballs that probably have a drug laboratory in their Pimpmobile's trunk.

After giving them about thirty minutes, I went over and had a peek on the other side, they had all gathered around this bitch and she was smiling like she had just won the fucking drug lottery . . . She even had one of the guy's hat on her head, this bitch was gone.

I stepped over to the group and I told them, "Excuse me guys, I'd like to speak to my friend here for a moment . . ."

They were drunk out of their minds, but they knew that they had this bitch copped.

I told her, "If you're still going with me, I'm parked where I always park, just down the street from the bar . . ."

Shaking her head, no, over the music she yelled, "Oh no, I'm ok . . . I'm definitely going with them! . . ."

They all looked at me and flashed their gold teeth . . .

"Ok," I told her.

"Thanks guys," I said and I got the hell out of their faces.

The next morning comes around and I see a leftover junker of a car with a load of clothes in it that looked like someone was living out of it . . . I guessed that it was hers, but she was nowhere to be found.

I had absolutely no idea where they took her, however, just to test my Pimpnological capabilities, I'm like, "This is my set . . . If the bitch is whoring in Memphis, I'll find her . . ."

Every week when I rolled back into town from a rotation out on the road I'd cruise down another track in my big truck and after about the third track I came up with her . . . They had the bitch working on Danny Thomas Boulevard.

However, reeling back to our long ago forgotten, Flash, after we had rapped into the wee hours of the morning and polished off the twelve pack of beer, Cochise went off to bed and Flash stayed with me.

Me being who I am, I wanted some pussy, so Flash took her clothes off . . .

I put on a condom that she has in her handy hooker condom collection and I start stroking, after a few minutes the condom breaks and I go to pull out of the pussy, but I can't. I stroke it about five or six more good times and I'm like, "Damn woman, that pussy is so good that I literally cannot pull out of it."

"I told you that I had some good pussy," she said as she laughed at me.

The next morning, I drop flash off and I'm in the wind on another crazy schedule.

Several months down the road, I'm parked in the same area, chilling out in my truck and someone starts beating on my door so hard that I think that it's either The Cops or The KKK . . . It turns out that it's Flash, she remembered my truck and when she climbed in she had a bit of an emergency . . .

Flash had somehow lost her car because it had broke down in the middle of nowhere and since she hadn't been able to sell any pussy lately she hadn't been able to get it out of the shop . . . So in desperation, she turns to me.

"I need to borrow about a thousand dollars from you man," she told me . . .

"I can't loan you a thousand dollars Flash, I'm about to the leave the country and go home to my wife . . . But you're more than welcome to ride with me to some whore spots that I know and try to work your way up on $1,000.00."

"Ok man, I've really got to get my hands back on my car," she said frantically.

I took this worn out old whore to every whore spot in the country to try to catch a date and she comes up with absolutely nothing and she's breaking me for beer and food every day, which means that she's breaking and Pimping me.

We roll into a swinging little trucker bar up in New York State, which was eventually shut down by the state for selling lines of cocaine over the bar, it was beer and dinner time, so we pile out of the truck and head in for some dinner, almost as soon as we get seated and order some drinks, Flash has to run off to the restroom . . .

When she leaves, some highly inebriated redneck from Alabama yells over at me, "Hey, that's a really nice lady you got there . . . Is she your girlfriend?! . . ."

"No sir, she is not . . . We're just friends . . . She's actually looking for someone to take care of her," I told him . . . His eyes lit up.

"If you'd like, I'll introduce you when she comes back," I offered.

He gives me a firm handshake and tells me his name and when Flash came back I introduced them, they sat together while I had my little dinner by myself and then before I went off to bed I told Flash, "If you're staying with him I'm leaving at 05:00am, if you're not there I'll leave your clothes in the parking space so that you can find them . . ."

"I'm staying with him tonight, but I'll be back at the truck by 05:00 to leave with you," she told me.

I'm like, "Ok Flash, but I live on a schedule and I don't have a pussy to fall back on if I lose my job, I really have to roll by 05:30 in the morning at the latest . . ."

Next morning, 05:00 hours rolls around, no Flash, 05:30 rolls around, no Flash. I knew where she was, dead asleep in someone's truck, but who knows which one . . . I took her bags, left them in the parking space just like I told her and I took off to make my delivery.

About a month later, same time, same place, I'm laying up in my sleeper and someone is banging on my door like it's either The Cops or The KKK . . . I get up . . . It's Flash, and she's mad as hell, sloppy drunk and crying hysterically.

"You dirty motherfucker," she yelled at me, as she leaned forward and almost fell on her face!

"I can't believe that you did that to me, you stole my clothes and left me in New York!"

Looking at her with a very disappointed expression, I told her, "Flash, you're wearing some of the clothes that you had in your bags when you were riding with me . . ."

"You stole my walky-talky," she yelled!

"Flash, I don't sell pussy at truck stops, so I don't need a walky-talky," I told her.

"If I had my gun I'd shoot you," she yelled in an increasingly more hoarse voice! After all that I'd done and spent to try to help her, I got pissed.

"Bitch, if you're going to shoot someone, you ought to shoot your damn self because you are the only one who's causing you trouble . . . I was laying up relaxing in my truck when you came and got me to go Pimping . . . I took you all over the Eastern United States and you couldn't sell a dime worth of pussy, but I didn't put you out of my truck in the middle of nowhere until you said that you were staying with someone else . . . And you fucked that up yourself, not me."

"Don't you ever ask me to help you again," I told her!

There are times in this life when it becomes necessary to put your shit in reverse and hit the gas.

I drove off and I've never again seen her.

THE MINIATURE
KINGDOM

I PHONED HOME one day, just to see how everyone was doing and instead of the nice, warm, soothing voice of my loving wife . . .

"Come home now!" A voice boomed over the phone . . . It was mom, and she was not happy.

"I'm coming," I told her, "I'm just trying to save up a bit more money . . ."

"Forget about saving more money, you have been telling me that you were coming over here for almost two years and it's getting really embarrassing, people are starting to say that I'm lying to myself and you're not coming . . ."

"That not true, I'll be there soon," I assured her . . .

"I've already bought your plane tickets, so you have two weeks to get ready, pack whatever you have and come home . . . I can't deal with anymore of this waiting and embarrassment . . ."

"Ok, mommy, I'll put in my resignation and hop a flight immediately," I told her.

When I announced to my rowdy trucker friends that I had been given an ultimatum of sorts and I was heading in, several of them didn't believe that I would actually go . . .

"Quit lying to everybody about leaving to go over to Japan, you know that you ain't goin' nowhere," one of my trashy redneck trucker friends blurted.

"I ain't goin' nowhere?"

"Why not," I questioned?

"It's my family . . . Why wouldn't I go home to be with my family?!"

"You've got it too damn good over here! You'll never be able to turn your back on all of this whoring and trashing! I see how much you're enjoying yourself, you can fool other people, hell, you might be able to fool yourself . . . But you ain't fooling me!"

"I'm actually not enjoying myself, I really want to go home, I miss my family and my kids are in kindergarten and since I'm not some welfare trash, drama junky ass Black bitch I have sense enough to know that they need both of their parents like they've always had, not just their ultra-dysfunctional mom, which is a totally jackass western feminist philosophy that has damn near made morticians billionaires and landed innumerable legions of young people in the cemetery."

When I finally turn in my truck and say my goodbyes to all of my trashy and normal North American Transportation Friends, I boarded a greyhound bus for Detroit where I took a cab to the airport to catch a thirty minute flight to Chicago followed by a flight to Seattle followed by a Flight to Tokyo and a final flight to Fukuoka where there was no one to meet me.

Since I spoke barely a word of Japanese, the rail police and I had to basically grunt at each other to try to figure out what the other was saying, however, we finally got mommy on the phone and they were able to figure out which train I needed to get on.

When I finally arrived in Minamata, after about a three hour train ride, my family was waiting at the train station for me . . . Ryo and Aka hadn't seen me in almost two years and Aka was blushing like crazy . . .

She was sooo happy to finally see her father.

We went directly to our little apartment and as an authentic gaijin welcome, I hit my head on the low door. Unlike the big Western size main Island metropolis', Minamata was real Japan and it was really small . . . For about three months I hit my head on literally everything.

I was so happy for us to have our own little place that I didn't know what to do and I was even happier to get back in mom's pussy . . . It was always a really wonderful place to be.

After introducing me to all of the neighbors in our building and giving them a small new resident gift, we went over to her parent's house, where I immediately apologized for the delay in coming to Japan and I thanked them for all of the support that they had given us when my in-laws had sent us cash on three separate occasions, including the plane tickets for Takako and the children to come home to Japan.

Before I realized it, Takako had took me to visit everyone that she knew, or perhaps everyone who had ridiculed her about me not coming to Japan.

We even went to my children's kindergarten, which had an environment that was so natural that the children moved around like a little breeze of wind or a school of fish, half of them were naked and some little girl was laughing as she dangled a little boy's penis . . .

It was by far the most healthy social environment that I have ever encountered, it could actually more accurately be described as a sterile environment; which I have lived many times, which is a community that is so clean and crime free that organized crime and drugs cannot gain a foothold because people won't support them or allow themselves to be recruited into criminal organizations and even the most horny or promiscuous women within the community are never referred to as whores and they subsequently don't act like whores or carry whore's energy.

Minamata was very different from Kumamoto, where I made what the Japanese found to be an astonishing two second determination that commotion that was claimed to be a gang war was in fact a drug war when I noticed tired adults and not a single child hanging around video game arcades. When asked how I had figured that out in two seconds flat, not wanting to explain that I was a grand inquisitor level Pimpnological decryptologist, I merely answered that it would be hard to explain.

The school's master, who was so rural that he didn't even speak the Japanese language, was a grandparent and master to all of us . . . I can remember that, upon hearing me refer to my wife as Takako, he chastened me to call her my wife. "Be sure to refer to her as your wife," he said.

I suppose that like many elders, he disapproved of the behavioral patterns that he saw in many young people.

Apparently, when I showed up at the kindergarten, some of the more mischievous little boys started teasing my daughter about being from Africa . . . She said that someone was teasing her because her hair was big and curly and not straight like the other children.

"A lot of other people say that your hair is pretty and they wish that their baby had hair like that," her mother told her. But this was a major crisis for Aka.

"Life is not a popularity contest," I reasoned. "There are people in this life who are going to totally worship you without knowing you and there are people who are going to totally hate you without knowing anything about you and you are absolutely no different."

"Everybody likes and dislikes somebody," I told her. "Now Aka, who do you dislike at the kindergarten?" This kid went on and on and on and on and on until I eventually stopped her, she named nearly everybody at the kindergarten.

"Aka, do you realize that you just named almost everyone at the kindergarten? If you don't like anyone at the kindergarten, then no one is going to like you," I laughed . . .

She didn't get the significance of what I was trying to tell her, but hating everyone was in fact one of her most Asian traits. I think that if my wife's father could have been there at that moment, he would have been beaming with joy, that would have surely been his proudest moment.

We also went to a restaurant and had Ikisukuri, which is raw fish that is cut so fast that when they serve it, it is still moving so that you know that it is fresh . . . Great for business, slightly petrifying for small children.

The next day, my youngest daughter had a play at kindergarten and it was literally petrifying to see the looks on the children's faces as they came out from behind the curtain and desperately scanned the audience for a family member as though their little lives would have ended if someone that they knew and loved didn't attend their performance.

The day after that, we went to Fukuoka to visit my wife's sister that had come to America during which she told her sister that she in fact had three children and then the day after that we went to an amusement park called Mitsui Greenland where there were lots of older Japanese men out on dates with absolutely beautiful and much younger Eastern European Women, which looked kind of suspicious, but everyone seemed happy.

We had several home parties at our apartment where we grilled meat together and when one of the little boys who attended a couple of them got full, he would get up and start dancing . . . I thought that the home parties were absolutely great, we had definitely not done anything like that when we lived in America and I only committed one cultural blunder when I got bored because I couldn't understand some of the ongoing conversation at one of the parties because I didn't speak anything other than pidgin Japanese at that point, so I got up and started to wash dishes . . .

When the Japanese guys saw me washing dishes at a home party they literally had a heart attack.

"What is he doing," one guy asked?

My wife laughed, "It's not uncommon for men to wash dishes in America."

Another guy, who was far less amused told her to tell me that I am not supposed to be washing dishes, that is women's work . . .

"Japan is a man's heaven," he said. "Don't ruin it!"

It was great to meet so many nice new people and we even met an interracial couple named Gavin and Aiko, who lived just outside of town. Aiko and my wife were coworkers at the time and we often went over to their place and socialized, our kids played together often and we had home parties together on several occasions.

Gavin's wife wasn't the prettiest woman in the world, but this chick had a figure that could make your head swim, she was built like a brick shithouse and having been a Marine, Gavin said that he had often had fights over her when they went out to military clubs as his fellow jarheads would try to make the moves on his wife and then tell him that he was lying when he told them that she was his wife . . . However, there were no such problems in the rural areas where we lived.

Southern Kyushu was so beautiful that it was totally amazing, it was so beautiful in fact that it looked staged like some kind of mockup of a natural area of the world that was so awesome that it couldn't possibly exist.

As I got settled in, I found out from my oldest daughter that my wife had been drinking and both mentally and physically abusing her . . . I had to get on my wife's ass about that and tell her to be careful about abusing the children and she immediately stopped it.

Since my wife's grand plan was for us to teach English together, I helped her teach English and we eventually found a job for me at a construction company to supplement our income a bit, especially after I started going to local bars and restaurants with Gavin.

As I worked at this construction company, where absolutely no one spoke a word of English, I learned several things about myself . . . Like the fact that I was extremely irritated by having dirt under my fingernails.

My job site boss was a very kind and interesting guy who had somehow communicated to me that he really didn't want to be a construction worker, what he really loved was cooking and he dreamt of becoming a cook, but he had been forced to be a construction worker because he had married into a construction family.

With the exception of slipping into a ditch because I walked too close to the edge of it, stepping on a few nails in my gigantic rubber boots and being hit with a hammer while an old guy and I were trying to drive a stake together, everything went pretty smoothly at work. I even had a couple of interesting experiences.

Like when we were laying some water lines and something went wrong on the site toward the end of our shift . . . I can remember the boss telling everyone to stop working, something was wrong that I couldn't understand . . .

So, we all stopped working and closed up and sealed off the site and went home for the day. When we returned the next morning, the boss pointed to a spot on the ground and told us "Dig right here." We started digging and a section of pipe that we had set had somehow popped loose.

I thought that it was totally amazing that the boss had went home and thought about it and when we came back the next morning, of all of the pipe that we had laid he had pinpoint precisely determined the area of the problem . . . I totally love positive solutions, I couldn't stop smiling.

On another occasion, when we were working a site in the mountains, it was a very hot day in tropical Southern Kyushu, so when break time came around, I took my shirt off and I was sitting there with the guys when an old woman came from a nearby house with tea and sweets for us.

We thanked her and as we sat there and ate them, she was looking at me like she was very fascinated.

"How nice," I said.

The underboss was like, "She came over here because of you . . ."

I looked baffled.

"She only came over here because you took your shirt off," he cited, as the rest of the crew laughed at me.

While most of the guys were extremely nice people, there was a quiet guy who was also quite cordial, except that he would jar the cement mixer whenever he lifted it over my head, which was quite deadly and very disconcerting. However, we eventually moved beyond that too to become socialites and I even brought him a few gifts from America when I made trips back to the U.S.

When socializing with common people, it was also very interesting to me that Japan is such an international country that people didn't immediately assume that I was from America because was Black . . . Very interestingly, people's first guess was that I was an Okinawan or from some of the nearby islands that surround Japan . . . There were in fact, many indigenous Black people, other than the Ainu, who lived in the islands that surrounded Japan long before Asians got there and there were even many Japanese who had nappy hair whom people told me were 100% Japanese . . . Prior to moving to Japan, I was not aware of that.

I also had a very strange experience in that, since we spent a significant amount of time with the other interracial couple that lived nearby, one day Gavin called me and said that he wanted to come over to my house.

I said fine, when he arrived and entered our apartment, he suddenly rushed in and ran all over the house very quickly checking the rooms and bathroom and then he checked the closets . . .

"What on Earth are you doing," I asked him? . . .

I had never seen anything like it and I had definitely not behaved like that on the many occasions that I had gone to his house.

"I'm sorry man," he said . . . "I thought that my wife was hiding in here."

I asked him why on Earth he would think that his wife would be hiding at our apartment and he said that she had been doing a lot of really strange things lately and he never knew what she was going to do next and he couldn't figure out what was going on with her, but she had been acting pretty weird.

I told him that I was a behavioral profiler and if he told me exactly what she had been doing, maybe we could figure out what was wrong with her.

He said that she had started running with strange people and wearing jewelry with strange emblems on it and, she had started staying out really late at night lately, she didn't want him to touch her and she had become rude and had developed a really bad temper.

Given the crazy bitches that I grew up with, I know all too well that women can be far, far, far beyond crazy, but it still sounded pretty strange to me.

"Has she started smoking cigarettes, biting her nails or lips or started scratching or scarring herself," I asked him?

He said that he hadn't noticed any nail biting or scarring, but she had started smoking cigarettes when she hadn't previously smoked.

All that I could conclude was that she had somehow gotten involved with drugs . . . It's all that made sense to me without knowing more about her and her behavioral patterns.

Within a few months, they had split like the average catastrophically disastrous military marriage and they finally divorced and he took the children back to America with him while she relocated to an undisclosed location and literally disappeared off of the face of the Earth.

As for my little relationship, though we were having quite a bit of fun initially, my wife had become bitchy and increasingly disrespectful . . . So I finally found out that she was in fact a woman and when she eventually blew up on me for nothing I told her that I was leaving Japan and going back to work in America.

She got in my face and told me that I wasn't going anywhere because I didn't have any money.

I was pretty pissed by now, and I told her, "You mean to tell me that there is a telephone on the wall that's working and I can't leave here . . . Woman I can be sitting in New York City Monday backed up to a dock getting unloaded."

"Let me show you something," I told her angrily!

I grabbed the phone and called my company and told them that I had gone into overtime already, my wife was acting a complete idiot and I needed a set of plane tickets back to work immediately.

My trashy outfit was like, "Son, we need you back here yesterday." And they took some information about the airport that I wanted to fly from and they found a way to use a freaking Comcheck to purchase a set of international plane tickets and I would pay them back at a rate of about $100.00 per week.

After I hung up the phone, my wife busted out crying.

After acting an absolute and complete idiot, she tells me . . . "You don't care about me at all," as she sobbed loudly!

I told her, "Woman, if I didn't care about you I wouldn't have spent years sending you my hard earned money and I wouldn't have come all of the way over here to Japan to live with you and the children."

"You know that I don't dish or take disrespect, especially not in my own home . . . So you acting a complete idiot with me is inherently detrimental to our relationship," I told her.

After this episode, I spent the next several years working in America and flying home to Japan for two or three weeks in the Summer and two to three weeks at Christmas and New Years.

Like any long haul trucker, I was rarely home, but I was able to provide a much better income for my family which was quite helpful in a country that is as expensive as Japan, which is touted to be the most expensive country in the world, next to Switzerland.

For years on end, all that I did was work relentlessly to provide for my family until my wife's behavior started to become so erratic that I fucked around and started to think that she was getting crazier than the totally out of this world crazy Black women that I grew up with.

At the very instant that that totally insane thought crossed my mind, I shut down everything and made what wound up being a twenty-five point list of everything that she was doing and then I used some of my tried and true Pimpnological behavioral profiling techniques to get a make on her and what my calculations yielded was that my wife wasn't just depressed or being a bitch, but that she had become what is behaviorally classified as a rotten whore, which is an extremely mentally unstable woman . . .

Though it is very hard for a person who has had a very ordinary life experience to imagine, as an individual who has been a highly dedicated student, researcher, advisor, teacher and ten toes stomp down disciple of the Pimping for well in excess of thirty years I can tell you that highly refined true master Pimpnological ideology in fact does have value and teach positive traits if one wishes to use Pimpnological ideals, capabilities and higher tactics positively.

Traits like extremely high levels of discipline, respect, both family and surrogate family values, toilette, consideration, calculation, both critical and dynamic thinking, insight, foresight, insanely high levels of self-motivation and the ability to see through virtually anything with fragments of clues.

Masters at my level of capability do not miss, we never have, ever. So I knew without doubt or question that my wife had become beyond crazy, however, what I hadn't figured out yet, was what was the cause of her steady degeneration into total insanity.

ARE Y'ALL READY FOR THIS?!

AS TRASHY TRUCKERS like to say, "You ain't gonna believe this shit!" But this is my story and I'm sticking to it and once you go down this rabbit hole, it's going to become crystal clear to you that you just can't make shit like this up.

My trip down the rabbit hole started exactly like the average trip down the rabbit hole of trying to save your marriage and do what is best for your children . . . Only this little trip had a horrifically sadistic twist, it was down a rabbit hole that had absolutely no bottom.

In about 2003, my oldest daughter had become a 7th grader and my youngest daughter was in the 5th grade and my wife was having what appeared to be the average crisis situation of being unable to manage the children by herself as they got bigger . . . She kept complaining to me that the children weren't going to school, which is a literal economic death sentence in Asia, so I shut down everything and again packed my bags to go home to Japan to help my wife manage the family.

Once I got home, to my surprise, not only was our apartment and absolute sty, but Takako had about 10 large trash bags of raw garbage stored in the room that she and the kids used to sleep in and they would just throw raw trash into that room and leave it there to mildew instead of taking it right around the corner to the garbage.

My oldest daughter had started menstruating and supposedly because they were more natural, they were using hand washable menstrual pads which they would hand wash and then allow to soak in a plastic bowl of blood red water that they kept on the floor in the shower room, which always had the door open so that visiting English students could see it.

I was so pissed about the raw trash that I almost had a heart attack, but I got the whole crew to their feet and we cleaned up the mess.

Before my flight had even touched down in Japan, my younger daughter's teachers had scheduled a parent-teacher conference with me because they had concluded that they couldn't effectively communicate with my wife. By this time, I spoke Japanese fluently, so I could meet their request that this parent-teacher conference be held with me alone.

When I got to the school, during regularly scheduled classes, the conference was with what appeared to be a relatively nice Japanese lady, who probably spoke some English, but I had become proficient enough in the Japanese Language that she didn't have to use a word of English.

She started out by telling me that, since I am not at home, there is a lot that I don't see that is going on with my family.

I told her that I had quit my job in America and had specifically come to Japan to try to resolve my family's problems.

She was quite pleased to hear that.

I informed her that I was well aware that my wife was mentally ill and that I had found out that my child wasn't going to school because her mother was telling her that it was ok not to go to school right in front of me and then immediately denying that she had said it.

I informed her that my wife had told me that the only two problems that she had in this world were me and the elementary school's principle, both of whom had very little physical contact with her and had absolutely no logical means of causing her such a high level of mental stress.

I told her that my wife had accused me of causing her to lose students at her English classroom when I wasn't even in the country for more than six weeks a year.

I also told her that for years I had thought that my wife was mad at me about something, however, I later discovered that my wife was in fact not mad at me, I had discovered that my wife was in fact slowly degenerating into insanity.

The teacher asked me if I had a few minutes to take a ride with her and I told her that I had as much time as she needed. The teacher took me to her car, drove me to my own apartment and she led me to our outdoor storage that each tenant had . . . We walked up to the storage and she told me to open the door.

I opened the door of the storage and to my surprise, there was my youngest daughter, fully dressed for school with her backpack on, sitting in a squatting position in the storage.

I was so shocked that I instantly had tears in my eyes, I had absolutely no idea that things had become this senseless.

"This is where your child hides every day that she does not come to school," her teacher told me.

I told the teacher that, I would keep Aka at home today and I would help her get motivated to start going to school regularly again, hopefully by tomorrow.

Later that day I sat my daughter down and explained to her that, though most everyone on the planet hates going to school, in the modern, highly technical world that we live in, if you grow up without an education you will have a very difficult time providing for yourself and your family and the only jobs that will be available to you are the dirtiest, most dangerous, lowest paying jobs that anyone can get and you will have a very difficult time affording anything.

I told her that, school would not be so bad if she involved herself in some of the more entertaining or academic activities that were available . . . "It will make it much easier to pass the time of day or grasp the concepts that your teachers are trying to teach you."

I also found that out that my older daughter had initiated a signed petition that had succeeded at making it against school policy for teachers to smoke at school, an accomplishment that, with the motivation of my crazy wife, she was very proud of.

They both wanted me to be proud of her too, however, upon telling me about her little petition to stop smoking at the Junior High School, my crazy ole lady asked me, "Aren't you proud of her," as they both presented beaming smiles?

However, to their dismay, I was in fact a bit upset.

"No, I'm not proud of her," I told them as their expressions soured.

"Cigarettes are drugs," I told them! "And people will kill you over their drugs . . . You're supposed to go to school to get an education, not to fight with the teachers," whom I later found out that she was also being belligerent to.

She had got so big and bad in fact, that when she got mad one day, as she walked past me, she knocked me out of the way with her pretty sizable shoulder and very rudely told me to get out of her way in Japanese street thug slang.

As an instant reflex action, I hit this kid so hard that I nearly broke my hand and I told her, "I'm your parent, don't you ever talk to me like that!"

As she lay on the floor crying, she said that she was sorry and I didn't have to do that.

I told her that I was sorry too, but I absolutely loathe bullying and disrespect, as I helped her to her feet.

After that, I never had to physically discipline my child again.

Her mother was totally pissed and wanted to fight me, however, she hadn't become that crazy yet.

I also later found out that she wasn't going to school either when having got the news that I had come home, the school called me one day, when no one else was at home.

"Is Ryo at home," they asked?

"No she isn't," I answered.

"Well she didn't come to school today."

"Ok," I told them, "When she gets back, I'll ask her where she's been."

When the kid paraded back home at right about the time that she would normally have come home from school, I told her that the school had called and told me that she didn't go to school . . .

I told her that if you leave here and give us the idea that you are going to school, go to school and if you're not going to school, we need to discuss it.

"Ok," she replied and we've never again had a conversation on the subject.

Miraculously, my daughters immediately started going back to school regularly and they continued to go to school regularly until they graduated high school in Japan and both of them eventually went to cosmetology school because they hated studying so much that they didn't want to go to the university like I strongly advised them to.

Another crisis came right out of nowhere when my crazy ole lady comes to me all panicky, excited and breathing heavily one day . . . I look at her with a blank expression on my face and ask her, "What is it?"

"It's Aka, you have to talk to her!"

"About what," I asked?

"She wants to run away from home."

"Ok," I told her, as I continued typing on my computer.

"What do you mean ok," she asked me?

"I mean, ok," I answered!

"This is really serious," she said excitedly, "Go and talk to her!"

I call the kid over to my room, which was also a classroom that my wife used to teach conversational English, and I'm not supposed to notice that my wife is standing off to the side of the door listening while I'm talking to her.

Looking at her with a very tired and bored expression, I told this kid, who is by now twelve or thirteen.

"Your mother tells me that you want to run away from home."

"Yeah," she said, with an equally tired and bored expression on her face as though she was already bored to death with our ridiculous conversation.

"Kid, if you want to run away from home, the door is wide open, I'll even help you pack before you run away from home and when you get back we'll all be right here where you left us and you can tell us your runaway story," I told her.

"Ok," she said. "You're really going to help me pack?"

"Sure I'll help you pack, I really don't mind you running away from home . . . I'm just interested to know what you feel that you have to run away from. Because as far as I can tell, you don't have anything to run away from, you people don't do dishes, you don't take out the garbage, you don't cook, you don't clean, you don't do laundry, no one is yelling at you or beating you . . . I really don't see what you have to run away from."

By now feeling pretty ridiculous, "I don't have anything to run away from," she told me. "I just want to see what's out there."

"Well that's perfectly ok," I told her. "And when you get back I'll buy a couple of cans of beer and some yakitori and we'll all gather around and you can tell us all about your big runaway adventure."

"You probably didn't know that I ran away from home three times when I was a teenager, twice from home and once from a foster home . . . But I had something to run away from."

Clearly surprised, her eyes got big and she started smiling.

"So when you get back from your big adventure, we can trade runaway stories."

"Is that it," she laughs?

"That's it," I told her.

When she walked out, my wife bolted into the room and asked me, "Why did you tell her that?"

"Why did I tell her what," I asked inquisitively?

"Why did you tell her that it's ok for her to run away and that you would help her pack?"

"I told her that because it's perfectly ok for her to run away and I'm more than willing to help her pack . . . My God woman, the kid just said that she wants to see what's out there . . . Running away isn't a problem, the problem is having somewhere to run back to if things get crazy or rough out on the streets and she's got that so she's covered."

"That sounds crazy," she told me.

"For the love of God woman, we live in the middle of nowhere, not Tokyo. There's nothing to happen to her down here . . . She'll make a run for it, get tired and sleepy, someone will take her in and give her something to eat and ask her her life story and then the police will bring her home in a few days . . . The end . . ."

"Oh, I guess that you're right . . . Think about it, once again you're worrying yourself over absolutely nothing."

We got over those little humps, but we weren't out of the crazy woods yet.

Being an insatiable female body and pussy lover, I am also a huge ass rubber and 100% all natural cotton panty lover.

One night, I'm lying in bed with my wife, lovingly rubbing her soft yellow ass, which was one of my favorite past times, when she abruptly got up and went to the restroom and came back to bed.

When she hopped back on the futon, I naturally started rubbing her ass again, only this time I noticed that her panties were wet, as I started feeling around, I noticed that her panties, especially her crotch, were in fact soaking wet.

I smelled my hand and it smelled like piss, I asked my wife, "Woman, why aren't you wiping your ass after you use the restroom?"

"Because I didn't want to have sex," she told me . . .

"You're a grown ass woman," I told her, "If you don't want to have sex, just say that you don't want to have sex." After I told her this, she just busted out laughing loud and uncontrollably . . .

And I thought to myself, "That's pretty crazy!"

Upon later discussing that episode with someone else, they said that that was a common symptom of someone who has Mad Hatter Disease, a Mercury based poisoning illness . . . But I still didn't get it!

Though she had always took care of our children impeccably, she eventually reached the point that she would take them places with their hair standing all over their heads and even take pictures with international visitors with her and the children looking homeless, even though between her working and privately teaching English, what I was sending home every week and our comparatively ultra-low, rural living cost, she was taking in nearly $4000.00 per month.

I spent nearly twenty years working as an international commercial driver to support my family, whom I sent $325.00 to $500.00 per week, but she eventually started telling me that she couldn't depend on me to support the family and the money that I was sending her wasn't helping her.

When I was at home, one minute she would ask me if it was ok with me if she went to the store and the next, she would get dressed and bolt out of the house and if I asked her about what time she would be back, she would become highly offended and treat me like I was some kind of domineering male chauvinist pig or something and when we would go somewhere in the car together she would run right through red lights as she let out a sinister laugh and when I said something to her about how dangerous it was she would get really mad and pull the car over and very rudely tell me that I could drive if I thought that I could drive better.

Before I returned to Japan, she had also very strangely started refusing to talk to me on the telephone when I called her international long-distance from America and she would spend up to twenty minutes breathing heavily on the phone like she was Darth Vader, as if she was mad at me about something but didn't want to say what it was and when I would ask her if she was mad about something, she would very bluntly say, "No!" And when I would finally hang up the phone and call her back later to ask her why she had done that, she would swear to God that she had never done such a thing and she would criticize me for falsely accusing her of acting an idiot.

For years she had refused to let the children come to America to ride with me for a couple of weeks or months during the Summer using what were clearly lame excuses, like they had to study and she eventually started asking me how much money she would get if I died in a truck crash, hounding me about the cost of coming home so much and accusing me of using the computer too much and costing the family too much money, even though I was only home for about six weeks per annum.

She had family photos of her and the girls on our refrigerator, however, when I would put up a family photo that had all of us on it, she would throw it in the garbage and burst out laughing.

As a highly educated and experienced Pimp, it had become graphically clear to me that, she and my daughters had become a girl's club and I was just a whore whose job was to stay out on the track until I was broke, busted or dead trying to make the cash to support their life of relative leisure and stay in a whore's place and out of these Pimp's business.

Since my wife taught English, she was often approached to translate various advertisements and documents into Japanese and when I was at home and they needed to do something highly complex, like make an English translation fit into the same space as a highly compact Kanji sentence, since I'm a writer, she would approach me to help her with these paid projects for which she would never give me a single penny.

This eventually became highly problematic because, when my children were in the second and fourth grades, I created an English language vocabulary learning system that was designed to help non-native speakers of English build vocabulary very quickly.

I chose the name Hatsuon Kyusaiho / Articulation Remedies for this learning system and I used it often when I was teaching English and since it was mnemonically designed with words that are pronounced very similarly it literally rhymed and was very easy for students to remember and they absolutely loved it . . . All that it needed was to be translated into the Japanese language so that we could monetize it to help finance our children's higher education.

To my dismay, in twelve years, Takako never translated the project, even though she would promise to translate the project to trick me into doing one of her translation projects.

Since this was an extremely vital potential means of financing our daughter's education, it was very important to me that the project be translated, but Takako diametrically refused to translate it because she said that no one would have any interest in it . . .

As I became increasingly desperate for her help translating the project, when she started taking on bigger and more complex translation projects she would use my desperation to get me to help her complete her paid projects and then she would laugh in my face and refuse to help me.

After several rounds of this, I told her that if she played me again it wasn't going to be funny and she promised not to play me again if I helped her complete this one really important project, so I helped her complete the project and once it was completed, she laughed in my face and refused to translate our project just as she had done countless times before.

Now if you're beginning to think that this bitch needs her ass whipped then we're pretty much on the same wavelength, because I had been thinking the same thing and after this bitch got into a phase of having me wash clothes and do dishes and clean the house while she was away doing God only knows what, while talking to me like garbage and absolutely refusing to ask the children to do anything and absolutely refusing to do anything that I asked her to do . . . I eventually pulled it on back for her and whipped the shit out of her and damn near choked her ass to death.

Since I am absolutely not about drama, during the full span of our twenty plus year relationship we never had any arguments and we only got into a single fight, because I absolutely refused to make domestic abuse a centerpiece of our relationship . . . Especially, not after I had figured out that she was in fact out of her mind.

When my wife eventually stopped teaching English with me just as the global economy started to slip into a recession and the construction jobs weren't there anymore, I took a job teaching English at a Japanese chain school that I later found out was rumored to be part of a huge trend of organized crime organizations using English schools, several of which were eventually closed down by the Japanese government, as fronts for money laundering operations . . . However, while I was at this particular chain of schools, I managed to have a bit of fun, make a little bit of money and get in a few extremely funny I'm not Yakuza, I'm Gyakuza, or just the opposite of Yakuza, jokes.

Since my crazy ole lady was driving me completely out of my mind, I took a company apartment in a nearby city and came home to Minamata on the weekends. When I moved into the apartment, we had company provided everything and I had to be at home to sign for the delivery of some of the larger utility items like the washing machine.

My apartment was right smack in the middle of a large entertainment district and I could hear heels clicking all through the night . . . It literally took me weeks to get to the point where I could get any sleep, because every time that I would hear a pair of heels, I would spring to the window to check out the woman who was wearing them.

Black cars, that were invariably driven by members of organized crime organizations, were always lined up all over the street as men in Black suits came and went and eventually there was a knock at my door and when I answered it, there was a guy in a Black suit holding some paperwork telling me that I needed to sign it.

I told him that I was sorry, but I couldn't sign his paperwork.

"So you don't care about this contract," he asked me, clearly disappointed?

"No," I told him, "It's not that I don't care about the contract, I can't read it and I don't sign anything that I can't read . . ." So he left and about an hour later my company calls me and asks me about the incident.

I told them that there are a lot of shifty people in the entertainment district around the apartment, so when a guy shows up in a Black suit, I thought that he was an organized criminal. The company told me that this guy was ok and they gave me an address to go to to sign the contract for delivery of some utility items.

So, I went over and apologized to the people and signed the contract.

A few months later, I received some mail that I couldn't read that looked like a utility bill for $50.00, however, when I went to the company that had sent it to me to inquire about it, they told me, "If you're a resident of Satsuma Sendai, the fifty dollars is for you, it's a one time payment that we send to everyone annually . . . It is a payment from the company for polluting the environment . . .

I had never seen or heard of anything like that in my entire life, however, the reason of the payment soon became clear to me . . . After a few months in the apartment all of my bodily fluids turned Black, mucus, saliva, semen, everything . . . It was very unsettling.

I also had, what was initially, one of the most freaky and anxiety inducing experiences of my life, simply trying to board a train in Nagoya.

I'm standing on the platform with everyone else waiting for a train, though I'm standing all alone as opposed to with a group. A train arrives, the doors open, I go to board and people start pushing me off of the train, so I push back against them and they push back against me and I push back against them some more and the doors closed and the train took off. At which point I notice that there is a pink sign with a woman on it on the door. Still slightly in anxiety induced shock, I ask myself, "What the hell that was about?"

After boarding the next train and finally getting where I was going and eventually discussing the anxiety inducing experience with someone else, a Japanese coworker who heard me talking about what happened laughed so hard that she had tears in her eyes and said, "You were trying to board the females only car of the train . . . In big cities like Nagoya, there are females only trains for women who don't want men feeling on them and rubbing up against them during rush hour . . ."

Now I'm thinking, "Females only train ha, just my luck!"

An even stranger experience than that, was that, once I had been assigned my given schedule, one of my classrooms had a little house next to it and as I worked in and out of there once a month I never really paid that much attention to it until one day, I drive up and there are about seven big, juicy Eastern European girls in what looked like a living room.

That got my attention, it was instantly crystal clear that they were being trafficked because they looked tired and some of them had rings around their eyes that were so dark that they looked like raccoons; although, big juicy ones.

Figuring that the girls hadn't had a good laugh in a very long time, I waved at them and then walked over and asked them if they were teachers.

The girls said, "What, teachers, did you just say teachers," as they all started laughing uncontrollably?!

"He thinks that we are teachers," one of them yelled, as they all continued laughing!

One of the extremely beautiful girls, who spoke very good English, said, "I've seen you here many times . . . Can I come up and see your classroom?"

"Sure," I told her.

She looked around to see if the coast was clear of mobsters and then she opened the ground level screen and climbed over the bannister and followed me up to my classroom.

"Oh my God, it's beautiful, I wish that I had a job like this," she said as she walked around and inspected the classroom.

"How did you get over here," I asked her?

She said that she was hanging out at a mall in her country and a man asked her if she wanted a job in a foreign country, "And that was it, I came to Japan."

After less than five minutes, looking worried, she said. "I had better leave . . ."

She told me the name of a club that she worked at and she told me that if I came there more than once, then I could arrange a date with her and we could go places together.

With the mess that I had at home, I really didn't need to add organized crime and government corruption to the equation, so I told her that I doubted that I would have the time and money to hang out at a hostess club.

Then she bolted out of the room and down the stairs like she was running for her life.

On the academic front, I also had some very interesting experiences.

The way that my schedule worked, was that I had a number of classrooms that I rotated into once a month so that all of the English students could experience a native English speaker at least once a month and they had the Japanese English teacher for the other three weeks of the month.

In each classroom we had what were the equivalent of classroom log books so that we could leave or receive messages from the other teacher that was running a particular class when they weren't there; which eventually proved quite interesting.

Since I rotated into several classrooms per day, in total, I actually had hundreds of students and all kinds of personalities. I had kindergarten girls who would ride into class on their grandmother's back and then when I got low enough, they would jump on my back and ride me around the classroom for the whole hour.

I had one girl who would spend the entire hour running around the classroom until her parents came back to get her . . . I was able to catch that kid once and listen to her heartbeat and marvel at whatever she was made of.

I had kids who were autistic and their parents were kind enough not to tell us, so they appeared to be slightly unruly . . . Which made me think to myself, thank God that I am not an abusive person, because it would have been a shame for someone to be abusing these children.

I had a short fat little girl that I couldn't pick up, even though I could easily pick up my normally sized wife . . . There was an excellent possibility that she was a little kung fu expert I concluded.

I had a boy who would get so pissed off if he lost a game, that he would just lay on the floor and tremor until his father came to get him and yell at him to get up and he'd spring to attention like a little toy soldier.

I had a girl that would cry for a few minutes after her father dropped her off, which made him think that she was crying throughout the whole class, however, I told him that she only cried until the games started then she would abruptly stop crying as she became obsessed with beating the other students.

I had a quiet boy whose father thought that his kid had a learning disability and couldn't keep up with the rest of the class. However, I told him that his son seemed completely fine to me . . . He just wasn't talkative, which as far as I am aware does not add up to a learning disability.

I had a little girl who kept coming over to me to tell me that one of the little boys kept looking under her dress at her panties . . . I ignored her initially, because I thought to myself that, what you're sitting on isn't even a pussy yet.

However, after she kept coming over to me and complaining about this kid, whom I never saw look under her dress once, I very embarrassingly stopped the class and asked the children in Japanese to please not look at each-other's underwear; which caused the entire class to burst out laughing . . . But it gained peace for the little girl and her panties because her little pal never looked under her dress again while I was there teaching.

I had a class clown who told me that, since I was brown, I looked like shit, after which his little buddies almost died laughing. However, when I told him that he was yellow and looked like piss, they laughed even harder which caused him to be embarrassed and a little pissed off . . .

After he took it upon himself to apologize to me, I apologized back and told him that there was really no need to apologize because I was a class clown too; which made him feel much better and as an added bonus, one of the little girl's parents bought me a six pack of premium beer for providing their daughter with a good hearty laugh.

We had a little boy who would spend the entire hour roaming the class and the teacher left me a note that told me to yell at him if he didn't pay attention . . . Which caused me to become severely pissed off and rip her message into as many tiny pieces as I possibly could as I thought to myself that, "People don't send their kids here to have us act an idiot with them."

Being unobservant, what she didn't realize was that the boy was a prodigy level genius, whenever I would present new material to the class, he would run up and look at a word or picture, touch it and run away to engage in his other interests . . . It took me a few rounds of this to figure out that this kid was in fact learning so fast that, not only other teachers but, his own mother thought that he was bad.

When we eventually had a parent observation day, in an effort to impress his mother, he correctly answered every question and aced every activity that we presented to him. His Japanese teacher was shocked because she thought that he hadn't been paying attention to anything, when in fact it was her who hadn't been paying any attention to him.

When his mother pulled me aside and asked me if her son was bad like people were saying, I told her that her son was too young to really be bad. What your son is, I told her, is extremely bored. I told her that her son was learning so fast that the other teachers thought that he wasn't paying attention and our fun and games with English classes were just too slow and repetitive for him, so he's not interested . . .

I told her that if she put him into a class where he was studying something that was extremely difficult to understand he would seem like a normal student because he would be drawn in to trying to comprehend it.

During my trips back and forth to America, people who knew us but hadn't seen Takako in years would often ask me how Takako was doing and I would tell them that she had evolved into a Chia Head and the women would always get pissed and angrily tell me, "Don't Call Her That!!!"

But I would tell them that she's absolutely and completely out of her rabbit ass mind and if she wasn't, I wouldn't call her that.

She started telling me that her parents said that she could not have any more children, even though she was over forty and had been married for more than sixteen years and when I asked her who she was married to, me or her parents, she would burst out laughing hysterically.

She very embarrassingly, eventually reached the point where she wouldn't teach the kids English or even let them sit in on her classes, even though she was privately teaching English at home and the children were failing English miserably at school, which drew numerous inquiries and complaints about what kind of parents we were from other parents and teachers and one day when I came home from the supermarket, I discovered the shocking reason why.

When I arrived home from a trip to get some odds and ends from the local grocery store one day, I very happily informed my wife that I had seen an extremely beautiful neighbor lady of ours, that I called The Goddess, at the store . . .

Upon informing her of this, she told me, "Oh, she's not married anymore . . . Two years ago her husband suddenly up and dumped her and the children and she never told anybody until just recently."

I quite literally froze in my tracks, as I thought to myself, "No one has dumped her and the children and disappeared into thin air!"

I was taken aback, I don't know why it had taken so long for me to put the pieces together but, somehow, this illogical abandonment helped me figure out that my wife, whose father had spent decades working with chemicals at Minamata Chisso Corportation, and innumerable other people in the community were a second or third generation of Minamata Disease who weren't born with deformities and who weren't being discernibly effected by the illness until they were in their mid-thirties.

All of a sudden, all of the really strange small business bankruptcies and divorces, including Aiko and Gavin's, made perfect sense.

MEDICAL DIAGNOSIS

ONE DAY, I WAS walking down the street in small town Iowa on an extremely rare day off from work and my feet got wet and I stopped dead in my tracks . . .

"How in the world are my feet wet," I thought.

I abruptly took off my shoes and they had holes in them, both of them . . . And I thought to myself, how on Earth did this happen?

When I got back to the truck, I started checking my clothes and low and behold almost every item of clothing that I owned had holes in them and then I had an epiphany.

I had told my wife that she was trying to Pimp the Pimp, but I had been absolutely wrong . . . She wasn't trying to Pimp the Pimp, this bitch had in fact Pimped the motherfucking wheels off of me!

One day I was at the bank and one of the more astoundingly attractive White women who generally looked at me like I was trash, suddenly beckoned me over to her desk.

"Have a seat," she told me.

I sat.

"I've been looking at your account and I've been wanting to ask you, who is in Japan?"

"My wife," I told her.

"I understand that she's your wife, but you really shouldn't be sending anyone that much money," she told me.

"My Lord," I thought to myself, "what if she knew about my severe dry eye, heart rate checks and bad pussy scare."

As I went down the road a few years earlier when I worked out of Arkansas, I noticed that my tongue was peeling . . . When I grabbed a mirror and looked in my mouth, my tongue was chalky White, it had several cracks on it and the flesh was peeling off of it.

Oh my God I thought, I must have eaten some bad pussy somewhere; a very common sentiment among over the road truckers.

When I went to the doctor, they said that they didn't know what it was, because it had happened too quickly after I estimated that I ate my last piece of highly potentially bad pussy at a whorehouse outside of Vegas.

"Virus generally have to have at least two weeks to incubate," the clearly disgusted young mulatto medical student told me.

"Well, I'm going home to Japan here pretty soon, they like fiber optic cameras over there, so I will see what kind of conclusion they come to."

Once I finally made it back home, I went to the hospital and I told the doctor exactly what had happened and that I'd went to the doctor in America and they couldn't figure out what was causing my tongue to peel, but they said that they were pretty sure that it wasn't a virus because the peeling happened too quickly after I took my last bite out of crime.

After having a quick look, "Sukareta dayo" . . . The doctor instantaneously concluded . . . Which means, that I was tired.

The doctor said that when a person is extremely exhausted they start to regurgitate stomach acid and that acid settles on the tongue and eats it . . . and his remedy was that I get some rest and hydration . . . No medical treatment needed.

Whew, good news, I thought that all of this lookin' for love in all the wrong places had finally caught up with me and some bad pussy was about to eat my ass to death.

Not long after I took a few months break and returned to work in America, I happened to run across Jody, whom I was not at all surprised to learn had become a strong, totally independent Black woman whom was an alcohol and anti-depressant addict who was, of course, crazy as fuck and drove her car like she was on crack.

As I was going down the road one day, the phone rings and it's my wife, who tells me that she has just sent my oldest daughter to Hawaii.

"What's Ryo doing in Hawaii," I asked her?

"She's looking for a job and she's planning to go to school there . . ."

"And how in the hell are we going to pay for that," I asked her, now totally pissed because no one has told me anything about sending my daughter outside of the country?!

"Don't worry," she told me, 'We don't need any help from you, we'll take care of it . . . You don't have to send us anymore money."

I was so pissed, that if she had been standing right in front of me, I would have knocked her nose out of the back of her fucking head . . . But all that I could do from that great a distance was bang on my steering wheel.

"Why didn't you tell me that you were sending my child to Hawaii," I asked angrily?!

"Because we thought that you would say no, so we went anyway."

Women really do have some kind of sadistic gift from God, because my blood pressure got so high that I had to pull over and take a nap and I don't even have high blood pressure.

Women, being the miracles that they are, these son of a bitches call me back about two weeks later to tell me that they miscalculated and that they would in fact need me to send $800.00 per month to Hawaii and $800.00 per month to Japan and they would need me to help my daughter get her social security card and birth certificate . . . After these dumb bitches had just told me that they would not need any help from me to do any of this.

I'm not a screamer, but now I'm yelling at people, "I thought that you motherfuckers just told me that you weren't going to need anymore help after you sent my daughter to Hawaii without telling me anything," I yelled into the phone, ready to break somebody's fucking neck?!

My wife, naturally, bursts out laughing because she's upset me.

"I never said that we weren't ever going to need anymore help," she said. "Calm down, we just made a miscalculation."

"You're telling me that you need me to send $800.00 to you and $800.00 to Ryo, how are you going to make it on $800.00 per month when you've spent years complaining that the $2,000.00 per month that I sent you was not enough?"

What I just said, must have been really funny, because my wife again bursts out laughing and she tells me, "I'll be ok, I never needed that kind of money."

What a revelation . . . I had been working myself to death while my merciless Pimp didn't even need the money.

As a first grader, several of my masters had told me that if a woman knows that you love your children she will use them to beat the Black off of you . . . At the time, it was the craziest thing that I had ever heard in my entire life and I discounted it, however, it was an insight that was by far more accurate than anything that I had ever read in the Bible.

By now, these bitches had become so ridiculously outrageous and had got so far out of check that after sending them $1,600.00 for two months, I was so mad about them constantly doing things that cost me money without having the common decency to tell me anything that I quit sending them money at all, so they had to pay for their hair-brained scheme for about eight months all by themselves and after my daughter eventually came over to America to ride with me in my truck for the first time since she was a toddler, we got to compare notes about what had really been going on at the house while I was out on the road literally killing myself to try to keep these people from starving to death and what I learned was of course astounding.

I found out that, as is usually the case when a guy is sending a bitch money, the kids were getting so little of it that they actually thought that I was just out riding around in North America and I wasn't sending home anything; when in fact, I had been sending 85% of my income to my family.

I found out that my loving wife had told the children that they shouldn't trust me or listen to me or tell me about anything that goes on at the house and she also told them that I could never send her enough money.

My little informant also told me that they had been wanting to come over and ride with me in North America for years, but their mother had always told them that I didn't want to see them.

And she told them that she had symptoms of Minamata Disease and one day she would die old and alone.

After I finally told my kid to write this stuff down, we wound up typing up a 64 point list of the absolutely and completely crazy shit that my little piece of heaven had been doing that spanned nearly two decades and when we finally made it back home to Japan in November of 2011 and immediately went to see a mental health specialist boy did we get a shocker that made my Black ass nearly turn White.

After looking at the list that we had typed in Japanese and sitting and patiently listening to our nearly twenty year dilemma, the doctor, who was a local Minamata Disease Specialist, swiveled around and reached onto a shelf behind him and started to thumb through a medical book while we were still talking and then he said, "Jin Kaku."

Over the years, I had become pretty good at speaking Japanese, but this word combo was a new one on me, so lucky for me, the doctor spoke pretty good English . . .

"Your wife has Multiple Personality Disorder, that is precisely what you and your daughter are describing to me," he told us.

"People who have this disorder lie a lot and they have no conscience and no ability to feel for other people."

I'm thinking, "That's my bitch, that's my crazy bitch right there!"

While I felt a sense of relief, as we were finally getting some real help, I was again taken aback and I actually felt totally stupid.

As a highly capable behavioral profiler myself, I in fact had noticed changes in my wife's personality, but what I noticed was so slow that I thought that they were merely mood swings . . . I would often think to myself that, one day I had a wife, then a mother, then a sister, then a daughter, then a child, then an infant, then a housewife, then a feminist.

My concept of Multiple Personality Disorder was a man going to bed with his wife and then having his wife wake him at four-o-clock in the morning asking him what he is doing in the bed with her, to which he replied, "You're my wife," only to have his wife reply, "I'm not married, I'm only a nine year old girl . . ." And thanks to my medical school graduate friend, I eventually discovered that that in fact is a dimension of Multiple Personality Disorder, however, it is not the only dimension of Multiple Personality Disorder.

I thought to myself, "Multiple Personality Disorder, no wonder this crazy bitch had never set her Pimp cup down, she had Pimped me until I was actually diagnosed and was being treated for severe exhaustion as a medical condition."

She had largely kept me from seeing the children until they were grown and if no one had stopped her, this crazy bitch would have in fact completely mercilessly Pimped me to fucking death.

True Master Pimps teach that, a wife is the ultimate pimp. One of the primary definitions of a Pimp is, someone who acts a fool with you and keeps you broke and if a wife doesn't fit into that category, I have absolutely no idea of who does. It is a totally irrefutable fact of life that as a man absolutely no one that you will ever encounter in life will act a bigger fool with you and keep you more broke than your wife.

I had known whores over the years who had been working on automatic for five years while their Pimp was in prison, but I had never heard of a whore, other than myself, who had been on automatic for more than 17 years . . .

"Hell," I thought to myself, "Me and this crazy bitch could be in The Guinness Book Of World Records!"

When we first met, I never even remotely imagined that we would have any problems . . . However, that was total ignorance on my part . . . If you have a woman, you have problems, that's a given of life and it is very interesting to me in hindsight that, for years we had had people that had known us since the beginning of our relationship call us and check on how we were doing.

I could always tell that these inquiries were not casual curiosity about whether we were doing fine or not, but people checking to see if were still together . . . For years, I thought that people were doing this because we were an inter-continental interracial couple, when in reality, people were checking up on our relationship status because they knew the history of Mad Hatter Disease and Minamata Sickness and they were in reality checking up on us to see if our children had been born with deformities or if my wife had lost her mind yet.

CURTAINS

WHEN I LEFT Japan in April of 2012, my wife was at her absolute craziest.

She would do shit that was absolutely crazy and then reciprocally be an emotional wreck.

For example, we got about a $3,500.00 loan for me to go back to America and work and hopefully be able to file a lawsuit against a government assisted organized criminal trucking outfit that had robbed countless others and I of well in excess of $140,000.00 each, which only added to the tremendous amount of stress that I was under in those days.

Since we had a bit more cash than we actually needed, we had enough cash to get her some new glasses.

I told this woman, "Takako, go down and get yourself some new glasses while we have the money . . ."

Being the wacko feminist, she absolutely and completely refused to buy herself some new glasses while we had the cash on hand solely because I was a man and I told her to buy them. However, she later went and bought some glasses after I got back to America and then she starts calling me ranting, raving and crying on the phone for me to refund her the money . . . I absolutely refused to send her the money and I reminded her that she had absolutely refused to go and get herself some glasses when I had told her to do it.

However, the straw that broke the Camel's back was the car that I had bought to get back and forth to work in Japan. I bought a Toyota Crown, which is a mid-level luxury sedan in Japan, and since I was going to be out of the country for several months and Kyushu is so humid, if I left home for six to eight months and nobody started the car the humidity would literally eat the car's interior and destroy its engine.

I told my gift from God that I needed her to start the car's engine and let it run for ten minutes per month so that the humidity didn't destroy our transportation investment . . .

Being a woman, as usual, it was far too much to ask.

"I won't have the time," she told me.

Then I'm like, "Woman, how on Earth do you not have the time to start the car and let it run for ten minutes per month . . . You don't even have to sit in it for the whole ten minutes, you just have to let it run and then come back in about ten minutes and turn it off."

"I'm not going to be able to do it," she retorted.

What a superwoman.

"Ok," I told her. "I'll find someone else to drive the car while I'm out of the country since you obviously can't handle that level of responsibility."

And of course, she busted out laughing.

While I was out shopping I happened to run across a bar hostess that I had known for about seventeen years and I told her about my situation with my crazy ole lady and I told her that she could drive the car for absolutely no cost, all that she would have to do is put gas in it and I would only want to drive it when I happened to be in the country and if I were to get my hands on a bunch of cash then I would buy my dream car and then we'd figure out what to do with it.

She was totally elated, she said that she and her daughter were looking to buy another car so that her daughter could get back and forth to work and this would keep them from having to spend the money for another vehicle and it would help her daughter to be able to save up for her dream car.

After giving her the car and informing my crazy ole lady about the arrangement, I hopped on a jet and headed back to work. The ole girl drove the car for about four months but, being that it was a full sized V8 with two air-conditioners, she gave it back to me saying that it was burning far too much gas which was costing her a small fortune . . . Which forced me into a situation in which I had to again deal with my crazy ole lady.

Being a raving lunatic, she once again refuses to start the car for ten minutes per month . . . In my mind, I'm thinking about this rotten whore keeping me absolutely penniless for the nearly two decades that I had been sending her money while neither she nor my feminist daughters could do a single thing that I asked them, so, I quit paying on the car.

Asia being Asia, when the Toyota dealer finally came to repossess the car, superwoman couldn't deal with the embarrassment or legal consequences and even though this rotten whore was hiding more than $250,000.00 somewhere, she didn't want to spend it or deal with the humiliation of turning to her parents for the $9,000.00 payoff money, plus the early loan payoff penalty, so she does what every rotten whore does and she tries to play the sweet little woman role and kiss and make up with me over the phone and promise me that she is going to store the car in her father's garage, start it for a grueling ten minutes per month and pretend like she has some sense, which never happens.

However, what no woman ever realizes is that, after a man has already become mad enough to brutally murder you, then the playing the sweet little woman who is pretending to have some sense role absolutely does not work . . . However, being a highly calculating Pimp, I played along with her feign of sensibility and decency that I know all too well doesn't exist, until she went down to the dealership and assured them that we would catch up the payments and got the car back and as soon as I was absolutely sure that the bitch had been able to reclaim the vehicle I change my email address and phone number and I didn't talk to this bitch ever again, which exponentially compounded the financially debilitating and humiliating effects of her hideousness.

Knowing that the bitch would again be talking about committing suicide, after about three years I left a message on her answering machine, just to see if she was still alive.

The crazy bitch messaged me back demanding a divorce and claiming that she didn't want to talk to me again after what I did to her. A day later, my youngest daughter calls me crying hysterically on the phone telling me that her grandfather had died and they thought that I had died or got married to someone else . . .

I reminded this idiot that, as usual with women, it was in fact their totally jackass idea for me not to come home when my oldest daughter got big and bad enough to tell me that I could just leave my own house and go back to America and I left and never came back. I told her that I was not dead or remarried, I was working as usual and I would have been at home, as usual, if it was not for them acting an absolute and complete idiot.

My youngest daughter just had to take a trip to America, so I wound up spending no less than $20,000.00 cash to get her over here, where she was to ride with me for about 10 months like her sister had done in 2010. Aka did pretty good for about two weeks during which, to my surprise, she informed me that her mother had been charging the cost of the children's high school fees, that I had already paid, back to my daughters and I found out that some total jackass had made her mother a teacher in the public school system, then she starts complaining about everything, running off and disappearing and talking to me like I'm a two dollar whore just like her mother was doing before I shit-canned her.

After I got beyond totally fed up with her disrespect and fool acting we eventually got into a fight and I almost broke her neck and scared her so bad in the process that she pissed all over herself, I suppose because I didn't prove to be as easy to beat up as her mother had since she had been in Junior High School and to keep myself from committing a murder, immediately after her 21 year old ass whipping I shipped her crazy ass right back to Japan so that she could be with her mother and all of her other crazy friends.

In the end, everything had been a waste and ended up completely going down the tubes, all of the love, all of the labor, all of the lectures and all of the responsibility had been for absolutely and completely nothing . . . All that I ultimately got out of the relationship was a great time with the kids when they little and some really great sex.

Sex with my wife was never a casual experience, it was always an amazingly wonderful experience in which I never felt that I could get deep enough into that pussy, even though I had been so deep in those panties that we pulled out three more people.

Given that I had been eating pussy since I was in kindergarten, it was very easy to turn my wife so far out to oral sex that she couldn't even believe her damn self.

And one interesting thing that I was able to learn from her was that pussy isn't the same everyday . . . When a woman is at the furthest point from egg day in her menstrual cycle, plugging into her pussy is like holding your dick in your hand. However, as my wife got closer to the point in her cycle when she could get pregnant, her pussy became something totally amazing that I could barely pull out of under my own strength.

I'm not really into crazy women, however, crazy bitch pussy is where it's at!

In the end, though I had been a totally responsible husband and father under the extenuating circumstances, I had ultimately been exploited and left completely without assistance on any level by the people like doctors, lawyers and politicians who were supposed to be there to help. And I had been robbed primarily because I just didn't have an ability to see how taking care of my family could be a catastrophic disaster that in the end would be all for nothing.

Though we got promises, we never got any help for my wife, because though there had been huge divisions among the various corporate, victim, governmental, legal and medical sides for half of a century, by the time that my wife's situation came up, there were no more divisions, everyone was on one side and given that they had heartlessly allowed nearly an estimated 80% or more of the Minamata Sickness Victims to die before they officially recognized and assisted Minamata Disease Victims, I believe that the consensus was that all parties involved just wanted everyone who had Minamata Byo to just fucking die and go away.

In my heart of hearts, I believe that this whole situation actually stemmed from the fact that, historically, the Kumamoto, Kagoshima Prefectural Border Region was one of the last hold outs that fought fiercely during the end of the Samurai Era and to get back at them, the people in Tokyo eventually used totally unbridled hyper-industrialization to poison more than four generations of people, animals and marine life for an estimated 258 mile radius of the Chisso plant with Methylmercury, which is widely known in Asia as one of the most poisonous substances on Earth and is in fact how silver chopsticks, which turn Black when they make contact with Mercury laced food, came to widely be used in Asia. Minamata-Chisso has since, changed its name, as everybody has resolved to make Minamata Byo just a blip in Kyushu's past history.

As for me, having bet the farm on my family, at 43 years old, I had to completely rebuild my life from scratch.

I had always had people ask me what it was like being Black and living in Japan, and aside from my wife robbing the holy living shit out of me, which constantly kept me broke and unable to properly reciprocate people's hospitality, it was absolutely great.

One of the general laws of hatred is that people hate people that they know, and as a Black man from Memphis, which may as well have been another planet, as far as Japanese hatreds went, I absolutely and completely did not exist, they hated other Asians from nearby landmasses and Islands.

I always analogized my situation as being at the end of a hate line that was a billion people long, my number was never coming up in my lifetime.

Another huge misconception about Asia, is that Asians hate interracial people, and that is largely absolutely not true, Asians are in fact fascinated by genetic anomalies, what Asians in fact hate is family dysfunction and since many interracial individuals are the products of military or binge relationships that invariably yield family dysfunction then it merely appears that Asians hate people with multicultural heritage.

By now, you have probably forgotten that this is a book about the omen of possessing pure Pimpnological energy.

I really don't believe that it was a mere coincidence that my marriage and family life eventually became so catastrophically disastrous, it happens to Pimps all of the time and I find it very interesting that, even if you don't have a single whore, if your level of dedication is pure enough for you to emit that, "If I be lifted up I will draw all men to me Pimpnological energy," then you will also draw the omen.